# UGGIE
## Testimonials

'He's the cutest dog!' – *Ellen DeGeneres*

'Uggie's right up there with the big ones.'
– *Harvey Weinstein*

'What a treat to meet Uggie. Oh, how I loved him!'
– *Goldie Hawn*

'Uggie inhabits a character and emotional range as
evocative as any of his human co-stars … He handily
outperforms Leo [DiCaprio] in *J. Edgar*, though might
not measure up to Clooney's work in *The Descendants*.'
– *S. T. VanAirsdale*, Movieline editor and creator of the
'Consider Uggie' campaign

'Uggie's the catch of the day!' – *Katy Perry*

'That was the best action I've had in years!'
– *Whoopi Goldberg*, after being kissed by Uggie

'Uggie gives the best performance, human or animal, in any film I've seen this year.' – *Lou Lumenick, New York Post* film critic who tried unsuccessfully to convince the New York Film Critics Circle to give Uggie a special award

'You have no idea how starstruck I am!' – *Gerard Butler*

'Uggie is wonderfully trained and talented. I'd like to see a special Oscar recognizing the achievements of animals.' – *James Cromwell*

'[Uggie] gave a wonderful performance … He's a great dog.' – *Martin Scorsese*

'This dog is a total scene-stealer!' – *Missi Pyle*

'Uggie was my shadow and my friend.' – *Jean Dujardin*

'Uggie was a star. It was a pleasure to work with such a pro. He became very important in the movie – much more than I had expected when I wrote the script.' – *Michel Hazanavicius*, director of *The Artist*

# UGGIE

## The Artist:

### My Story

**BY UGGIE**

with
*Wendy Holden*

HarperCollins*Publishers*

This memoir is based on my recollection of events, which may not be exactly as others recall them. Where human conversations cannot be remembered precisely, I have re-created them to the best of my canine ability. Where people or animals need to be protected, or to avoid offence, I have altered names. Any mistakes are my own.

First published in 2012 by HarperCollins

HarperCollins*Publishers*
77–85 Fulham Palace Road
London W6 8JB

www.harpercollins.co.uk

1 3 5 7 9 10 8 6 4 2

A catalogue record for this book is
available from the British Library

ISBN: 978-0-00-749290-9 (hardback)
ISBN: 978-0-00-749291-6 (ebook)

Printed and bound in Great Britain by
Clays Ltd, St Ives plc.

**MIX**
Paper from
responsible sources
**FSC** **FSC™ C007454**
www.fsc.org

'I class myself with Rin Tin Tin. At the end of the Depression, people were perhaps looking for something to cheer them up. They fell in love with a dog …'

*Shirley Temple*

*For Reese, my love, my light*

WITHOUT WONDER AND INSIGHT
ACTING IS JUST A BUSINESS. WITH IT,
IT BECOMES CREATION.
*Michael Chekhov*

The humans were excited. With my keen sight and sense of smell, I could tell that something was up. My Facebook and Twitter pages were abuzz, and everyone had been prepping for hours. Mom Mercy had been to the nail salon and Dad Omar had shaved – inexplicably – twice.

Smells of soap and shaving foam, perfume and hairspray overpowered my nostrils, until I sneezed them clear.

Having endured another pawdicure and full body grooming, I jumped onto my skateboard and completed a few circuits of the swimming pool, to loosen up. Sniffing the air, I detected a whiff of squirrel and spotted it chattering nonsensically as it did its high-wire act on the telephone line slung high above our back yard. Flying into a rage at the sight of that bushy-tailed trespasser, I abandoned my board and barked until my throat ached.

No amount of coaching could rid me of my intense dislike of squirrels, birds, cats, and – oddly – zebras, but more on that later. I was, however, getting a little long in the tooth to keep chasing vermin; or anything else for that matter. My 60 years (in human terms) of performing in commercials, motion pictures, photoshoots and animal shows were beginning to take their toll. My bones creaked, my legs trembled, and Dad had retired me from water-skiing, which was a shame, because I was both a speed freak and a water lover.

I was born an Aquarian in February 2002, to two Jack Russell parents. According to an astrology channel I watched with my fellow couch potato Gordo (an American bulldog and a Leo), those born under the sign of the water carrier are intelligent seekers of life's mysteries, whose quest is to be unique. We are loyal, honest, inventive, and original. On the down side, Aquarians can sometimes be exhibitionists.

I qualify on all counts.

I can recall very little about my puppyhood. I think I met my father once when he came to sniff dispassionately at me and my sprawling siblings. All that I remember of my mother was that she was gentle and nurturing; the smell of warm milk would forever remind me of her. Sadly, I was plucked from her teat early on and sold to the first stranger to pick me out from the litter.

Banishing that unhappy memory, I sprawled on the deck with my legs splayed flat on the cool concrete. I was sweltering under the Californian sun after my blow-dry. I toyed with the idea of jumping into the pool to cool off, but I suspected that wouldn't be a popular move, especially as I was sporting a bow tie made especially for me by Chopard.

It's not every day an actor sports
a $60,000 bow tie.

Featuring an 18-carat gold bone inscribed with my name, the $60,000 adornment was mine for one night only, before being auctioned off to benefit an animal rescue charity.

Although I was grateful to Chopard and fully applauded the sentiment behind the gift, I still scratched at the floppy black satin to loosen it a little. I've never been a fan of getting dressed up like a human. I just don't see the point. What is wrong with a little nudity, when you are in such great shape as I am? Admittedly, I've seen a few Shar Peis that could do with a burka, and every full-male Great Dane I've met could benefit from some support underwear, but generally I believe in going *au naturel*.

At least my bow tie made a change from one of the more schmaltzy leashes and collars my adoring fans insisted on sending me. There were scores of them in my closet – red ones and green ones, pink, purple, and blue. Several were smothered in bling and quite a few featured little bones or stars.

My favourite was the Palm Dog, a sturdy leather piece with a tastefully engraved inscription. A panel of international film critics awarded it to me in 2011, in lieu of a human Palme d'Or, at the Cannes Film Festival in France. Yes: France. Where I shall one day pad my paws along the famous Croisette with the best of them (and, no doubt, leave a few choice p-mails for my fans).

The Palm Dog was my first major award and therefore my most highly prized. Even Lassie didn't get one of those, although, to be fair, the concept of honouring four-legged actors hadn't been dreamt up back then.

As I lay panting by the pool wondering what theatrics I might have to perform for Dad later that night, I felt my stomach rumble. It had been more than an hour since my last meal, and that could only mean one thing: 'Lights! Camera! Action!'

Not that I minded, really. Being in the spotlight appeals to my exhibitionist side.

I especially enjoy showing humans how to perform a stunt properly or deliver a scene in a single take. I listen to my cues from Omar, play my part, and aim to be 'right on the money', as he calls it. On set, directors love working with me, because I am usually the last character they have to worry about. Often, though, something is still not quite right (mostly down to human errors) and we have to go for another take.

My tummy rumbled once more. Everyone was getting so animated about this Oscar guy. I didn't know who the heck he was, but I knew one thing: if he didn't have a sausage treat for me in his pocket, then I'd give him a trick to remember. My finale might well include a special award that couldn't easily be cleaned off any carpet – not even a fancy red one.

Better than any of these thoughts, however, was the hope that my beloved Miss Witherspoon might be at the evening's big event. It is no great secret in Hollywood that 'Miss W.' and I forged a unique bond on the set of my previous movie, *Water for Elephants*, which also starred *Twilight*'s heart-throb Robert Pattinson.

I never really got what all the fuss over Mr P. (or 'RPattz' as his fans called him) was about by the way. On any given day, there'd be hordes of young female humans screaming for him at the studio gates, but the supposedly smouldering biped couldn't even skateboard as well as me!

The chance to smother Miss Witherspoon's face in my trademark slobber? Now that is worth a howl or three.

As someone born in the sign of impulsive Aries, she is highly compatible with my cool Aquarian nature. Ours was one of spontaneous attraction. It was literally written in the stars that we were destined to enjoy what I hope will be a deep and enduring love. Whenever I came into her orbit, the incandescent smile she gave me was even more captivating than a slice of pepperoni. To preserve my movie-star demeanour, I frequently had to be pulled away.

In spite of some of the more scurrilous gossip in the Tinseltown press, I never once tried to hump her leg (although I do confess to slipping her the tongue once, during an off-set smooch). Even when she was clad in little more than a sparkly bikini as she rode bareback on a circus horse, I remained entirely chivalrous, as befitting a middle-aged gentleman, in the company of a lovely Louisiana lady.

Charlize Theron, Tilda Swinton, Katy Perry – they have all vied for my affections at the many awards ceremonies to which we have been invited since my latest movie, *The Artist*, had its first sniff of success. Heck, even George Clooney made a move on me, but there is only room for one Hollywood beauty in my terrier heart.

I sighed and rested my head on my paws.

'Oh Reese,' I pondered dreamily, 'why haven't you called?'

## ACTING IS STANDING UP NAKED AND TURNING AROUND VERY SLOWLY.
### *Rosalind Russell*

Dad Omar wandered out into the yard in the tux he'd had to wear so frequently of late and whistled me over to him. I sprang to my feet out of a combination of loyalty and love (and in the hope of a reward). I was not to be disappointed.

As I gobbled up a few bacon bits and allowed him to rub behind my ears with hands that smelled of aftershave, I thanked the Dog Stars for the nine years he and I had spent together.

Omar was a good man, in spite of publicly professing that his childhood hero had been Lassie. Most importantly, he'd saved me from being dispatched to a pound. I'd never seen inside one of those infamous dog gaols, but I knew they were places where a troublesome puppy such as myself might easily have vanished for good.

My previous human had decided to give me up, all because I'd rid the world of a pesky cat. I'll reveal more about that later, but what I can say in my defence is that, like most young pups without the steadying influence of a father figure, I got into some trouble. I was too young to know the difference between right and wrong.

Think Robert Mitchum.

Fortunately for my furry hide, Omar heard that I was headed for the pound through a friend who knew he trained animals for a living. 'Jack Russells are the best,' Omar told her. 'I'll foster this little guy for a while and see how he responds.'

The man who was so ready to get rid of me never thought I'd amount to much. 'That dog's a cat killer who barks all day and runs after cars and birds,' he warned.

He said that last part like it was a bad thing.

In what I considered to be Omar's greatest moment of genius, he insisted, 'Uggie only acts crazy because he's so smart.' That's when I knew that my new Dad was the human for me. From that moment on, we had little need for words, he and I; we understood each other perfectly.

It was then that my devotion to him began, for here was truly a man with a dog heart.

Waiting by the pool with him the night we were due to meet 'Oscar', my body relaxed as Omar caressed me. I pricked up one ear and then the other as he began to talk to me in that odd jumble of sounds humans use to communicate. His Colombian accent has a more exotic twang to it than my own Southern California drawl or Mom's lilting Florida way of speaking. If

Dad spoke too fast, not even Mercy could understand him, but I still usually picked up most of it.

'This is a big night, buddy,' he told me with a grin that could light up an entire movie set. 'It's bigger even than the Golden Globes.' He chuckled at the memory. 'Man, Ugg, when you lifted your paw and placed it on top of that award, you really freaked us all out. It was way too human!'

**Staking my claim to our Golden Globe.**

I cocked my head and registered a few more familiar phrases like 'good boy', 'gentle', 'stay', 'cameras' and 'pup-arazzi'. I was disappointed not to hear Omar speak my favourite word of all – 'sausages' – but hoped that was just an oversight on his part.

I wagged my tail wildly at the name 'Jean', my co-star in *The Artist* who'd become like a brother to me. Mr J. and I had even played together for a few days in the back yard of his palatial Los Angeles house before filming began. It's common practice among us actors to get acquainted first, so that the chemistry is sizzling once the cameras start to roll.

What I quickly learned during those happy days teaching Jean my most important routines was that the smooth-talking Parisian had originally started out in comedy and cabaret – just like me. A Gemini by birth (but an Aquarian by nature), he'd already been in one dog movie entitled *Un Homme et son Chien*, albeit with a *très* inferior Jack Russell. And, yes, that was French, which I had to learn quickly, for Jean spoke little English back then.

On what I came to think of as the 'O' night when I was to be reunited with him, a big black limousine pulled up outside our house. The driver leaned lazily on his horn. Mom emerged from the house looking especially well groomed, and my nose twitched wildly. She smelled like gardenias on a hot summer's night.

She and Dad kissed my six-year-old 'sister' Terry goodnight as she lay snuggled in her bed surrounded by her favourite soft toys. Mom gave the babysitter her cell phone number and then she and Dad took turns to pat the other dogs goodnight.

Dash, my chief stunt double in *The Artist* and other movies, lay in his basket and barely lifted a lazy Jack paw. Jumpy, the talented collie mix who specialises in extreme high jumps, freestyle painting and flyball, raised his sleepy head and winked me a goodbye (yes, really). Julio, the mathematical English bulldog with his copious folds of skin and permanently quizzical look on his face, panted a husky farewell.

Gordo, my best buddy in the world next to Omar, got up from his bed and kindly slicked down a couple of unruly hairs on my coat with a friendly, wet tongue.

Big Popeye lay spread-eagled on his bed in that American bulldog way of his and eyed me menacingly. He was more than three times my size and had the breath of a skunk, but we'd always played roughhouse together and been contented housemates.

That was until he wormed his way into the affections of my beloved Miss W. on *Water for Elephants*. Even though he only had an insignificant part in that movie (and certainly didn't warrant his own temperature-controlled trailer like me), he must have done something to capture my true love's heart.

'Oh, hi Uggie! Where's Popeye?' Reese would croon whenever Omar and I arrived for a scene. If the answer was that he wasn't there that day, her face would fall.

I don't know what that bad-breathed bull-baiter did to bewitch my movie star (could it have been that he capitalised on my having to play a bitch in that film?), but I could never quite forgive him for trying to steal my beautiful Southern belle from under my nose.

A veteran of more than five movies, Popeye also earned his keep as a 'safe attack' dog and professional dock diver. He may have had slightly more film experience than me, but I was streets ahead of him in the commercial genre, having advertised everything from cars to beer with acclaimed panache. I was also the undisputed skateboarding star of the latest Savanna dry cider commercials.

Popeye was good, but not that good, and the three-year-old lummox was clearly growing tired of me stealing the spotlight.

When it was Popeye's turn for a farewell petting from Mom and Dad, he shamelessly over-acted and flashed them his saddest expression with a full droop of one ear and a downturn of his flabby mouth.

I am – I've often been told – a fine example of a classic hound originally bred for fox-hunting in the shires of Old England. Reminded of my own high status, I trotted breezily past his bed and headed for my waiting limo.

Popeye, whose origins were Spanish, watched and waited and, to my great indignation, shifted his 90-pound bulk and let a ripe one go, making my nose wrinkle in disgust.

Man, I was going off that dog.

From the smell of him, the feeling was mutual.

**3**

## I'VE SEEN A LOOK IN DOGS' EYES, A QUICKLY VANISHING LOOK OF AMAZED CONTEMPT, AND I AM CONVINCED THAT BASICALLY DOGS THINK HUMANS ARE NUTS.
### *John Steinbeck*

For all the respect due to Lassie, I never quite got all the fuss. To my mind, Rin Tin Tin was a far superior actor and even Moose – the dog who played 'Eddie' in the long-running TV series *Frasier* – had more going for him.

Moose was a personal hero of mine, actually. Not only did he share my terrier good looks but he'd been rejected by his first human as a pup, just as I had, for being too much of a handful. I don't believe he had feline felony on his paws like me, but he did escape a lot and climb trees. That a boy! Flown to LA from his home in Florida, he was coached up for the movies and within six months had been accepted for the coveted role of Eddie.

The rest, as humans say, is history.

Moose was predisposed to aim for the good life and seek to make a difference in the world. His innate over-expressiveness could sometimes ruin his scenes, but he compensated with what I consider to be his finest trick – the deadpan stare. It was always amusing to witness humans capitulate to a higher intellect. Moose undoubtedly paved the way for character canines like me, and I will be ever grateful to him for persuading the crew to introduce liver pâté and sardine oil for any licking scenes.

Rin Tin Tin was a hero even in the human sense of the word. That shell-shocked soldier had been saved as a pup from a bombed-out French battlefield during the First World War and transported back to what was then 'Hollywoodland'. A true rescue dog, his first starring role in 1923 allegedly saved Warner Bros from bankruptcy. Within a few years, he was receiving votes for Best Actor at the Academy Awards. Like the rest of us Hollywood hounds, though, he came to know the sting of species discrimination and was doomed to become a Red Carpet Reject.

Rinty, as he was known to friends and family, also made the transition – difficult for a dog – to the wireless, and he starred in his own radio show for CBS. American audiences took his immigrant status to heart, and he was the first dog to be honoured with a coveted terrazzo and brass star on the Hollywood Walk of Fame. He also paved the way for lucrative endorsement and advertising deals, for which I shall always think fondly of him.

He even died like a movie star: aged thirteen and in the arms of 'the Blonde Bombshell' Jean Harlow, which I always thought ironic. A bombshell marked the beginning of his life as well as the end of it, but enough of my puns.

Lassie, by contrast, was an imposter. Born into a pampered life in California during the Second World War, he wasn't a bitch at all but a dog named Pal. The American icon, whom Omar watched devotedly on the black-and-white television in his childhood home of Barranquilla, Colombia, tricked thousands of his fans into thinking he was a silky-haired dame.

He should have been renamed 'Lass-he'.

His boastful human also claimed Pal had a star-studded pedigree and was descended from England's first great collie 'Old Cockie'.

Cock-and-bull, more like.

Although Pal had an early penchant for chasing motorcycles (for which I have some sympathy), I heard that he was hired by MGM initially as a stunt dog but quickly made his mark. There are so many apocryphal stories about Lassie, but one of them is that when the she-dog originally booked for the role refused to swim across the river, he waded in and won the part from under her quivering nose. (I call her a 'she-dog' because I never really took to the word 'bitch'. To me, it had all kinds of negative human connotations and none of them appealed to my genteel nature. A female cat was known as a 'queen', a female horse was a mare, and there were sows and dams, ewes and does – all of which have a far softer tone to them than 'bitch'. If a lady wolf is known as a she-wolf, I think a lady dog can be a she-dog.) Whatever her moniker, the female who was supposed to be Lassie failed her first test and loped off in shame, while Pal went on to become a major star and the second dog to be honoured with a star on the Walk of Fame (on which I've left p-mail and a fan letter or two).

No matter how much he may have achieved in his canine career, I could never forgive Pal for what I viewed as disloyalty. A stunt dog doesn't make the star his fall guy, even in what has always been recognised as a dog-eat-dog business.

I try to set aside my ambivalence, though, in respect for Dad's feelings, because Pal stamped a paw print firmly on Omar's boyhood heart.

'I watched Lassie movies with my brothers when we were kids and loved them,' he told me. 'When I was 11 years old, I trained my first dog, a German shepherd named Kaiser, to do the same routines – even jumping through hoops of fire. My older brother Nelson trained dogs for police and protection work, and he taught me most of what I know. But it was Lassie who really got me started. *Lassie* was my movie. I loved everything that dog did.'

If I'd been able to speak human, I might have told Dad the truth about Lassie, and pointed out that – like Rin Tin Tin – the original star was replaced time and again, as the brand continued but the animal actors grew old and died. Then again, maybe I wouldn't, for it would have been cruel to lift my leg on the candle Omar held for the so-called 'Wonder Dog'.

Aside from his soft spot for Lassie, Dad was an intelligent human who'd had a profound love of animals since childhood. People used to bring him injured birds, dogs, rabbits, chickens, even a bear and an alligator, and he'd fix them up and teach them tricks.

'Every night when I got in from school, I'd hurry to tend to my animals and then I'd run up on the roof of our house and lie on my belly looking down on them all in the yard, studying their behaviours. I'd dream about going to the United States one day, and maybe even working in Hollywood with them. I'd only come back down from the roof when night fell.'

Omar had done really well for himself since leaving Colombia as a 15-year-old with his family, in search of the American dream. Entrusting his beloved Kaiser to the care of his brother-in-law (where he was to die young, sadly), he moved to Baltimore first and continued owning and coaching animals all the way through high school.

'I found myself a Newfoundland puppy and named him Kaiser, after my old dog. I read up everything about Newfies and how they were trained to swim and run and drag the nets in for the fishermen, so from the start, I ran with that dog and I worked him like an athlete,' Omar said.

'I trimmed his coat and kept down the fat. He became so muscular that he didn't even look like a Newfoundland. I trained him to rescue a crying baby doll from a floating basket, and when I took him to the lake one day with his brothers and sisters and they all rushed into the water after him, he spent the next half hour "rescuing" them all and then barking at them to stop them going back in. The protective instinct in him was that strong.'

The one thing Omar taught Kaiser to do, though, was something he has never been able to teach another animal to do since. 'I saw a scene in a Lassie show where the dog leapt straight up in the air out of a drain and wanted to see if I could get Kaiser to do that. I started by making hoops with my arms and teaching him to jump through them sideways. Then – after many, many hours of training – I got him to jump straight up into the air from a standing position through the hoop of my arms without touching them or me. People couldn't believe what they saw.'

Poor Kaiser was to suffer a tragic end – poisoned when Omar left him in the care of a friend. He could never bear to name another dog Kaiser again.

## LOVE THE ART IN YOURSELF, NOT YOURSELF IN THE ART.
### Constantin Stanislavski

When Dad left school and realised that he could make a living out of training animals, he moved to Miami, Florida, and set up a business there.

Like his big brother, he trained attack dogs and did a lot of street performing. He branched out into commercials and a few movies, too, sometimes joining his animals in front of the camera to play the part of a police officer, dog handler, or gangster.

Omar would probably have stayed in Florida but for Hurricane Andrew, which in 1992 well and truly cocked its leg on his life there. Having refused to evacuate from the area if it meant leaving his animals, he sat out the tempest and eventually emerged with them to see what was left.

'It looked like the end of the world,' he recalled. 'I never wanted to experience that again.' In true canine style, he picked himself up, dusted himself off, and started over – this time in Los Angeles and with a new Jack Russell in tow.

'Andy' was found barely alive in the debris as a newborn pup, so Omar named him after the hurricane that nearly killed him. He trained him up for commercials and print ads, as well as a few TV shows – or what I like to call 'Doggy Drama'.

Omar's first few bookings in the late 1990s were with some of the German shepherds he'd successfully trained for the sport of Schutzhund, which involves tracking, obedience, and protection. One day, he was hired to take one of his dogs to a motel for a magazine spread, but was given no more information. When he arrived at the run-down establishment on the outskirts of the city, he was shown into a room and came face to face with Sharon Stone, who was there to pose as a woman being arrested.

'I couldn't speak,' he said. 'I was one of her biggest fans. That was, until I realised she didn't like my dog.'

One of Omar's luckiest breaks came during a casual stroll along the California shore. 'I was on Venice Beach and saw a Jack Russell playing with a skateboard,' he recalled. 'That dog was going crazy. He was barking and biting at it and putting his front paws on it and trying to run with it. I watched him and I thought, "Hey, I could train a dog to do that!" I had Andy at the time and a Jack named Pete, who turned out to be really great at skateboarding. With practice, he got better and better and ended up being able to negotiate curves and jumps. He was amazing. Other people saw him and started training their dogs, too. As far as I'm aware, though, I was the first. I renamed him "Extreme Pete".'

Now, Extreme Pete was what I call a demi-dog. He should have been called 'Prometheus Pete' for all he sparked in the field of canine invention. Omar taught him to skateboard down stairs, rip up ramps at skate parks, and even bow his head while rolling along at such a pace that no human could keep up with him. That little guy was truly a swashbuckler in the mould of Douglas Fairbanks Jr – on whom Jean Dujardin was later to model his character George Valentin in *The Artist*, incidentally.

Gordo, Pete, me, and Dash
in perfect sync.

Like 'George', Douglas Fairbanks Jr began his career in silent movies playing daredevil roles, and was then faced with a dilemma when talking pictures came along. He was one of the few to make the transition. Rin Tin Tin was not so lucky. Even though the handsome German shepherd had been the biggest box-office star in the country, paid more than eight times his human co-stars, he couldn't speak. When talkies arrived, he fell from favour.

Douglas Fairbanks Jr, on the other paw, spoke beautifully and – maintaining his position in the firmament – went on to become an all-American hero with the advent of the Second World War, earning medals from the US Navy, France and Britain for his role in the amphibious assaults on the French coast.

After Omar coached him to water-ski, Extreme Pete made a few amphibious assaults of his own, as well. That dog was fearless! With no sense of impending danger, that all-white Jack would cling to his surfboard like poop to a scoop. The only thing he didn't much take to was wearing a cumbersome life vest. Who wants to consider the risks when you're ripping through the water like a dogfish?

By the time I wriggled my way into the world and was named 'Uggie' by my first humans (I'd have preferred Duke or Earl, as befitting my heritage), Pete was already a living legend. He and Andy were to become my fraternity brothers and my greatest role models – Pete in the field of extreme sports (although I was never quite able to match his prowess), and Andy in the craft of acting (which some say I have since surpassed).

Unfortunately, Pete had a single, fatal flaw. He was crippled by stage fright when it came to performing in front of live crowds. Ears flat, he completely lost focus and became fearful of applause and shouting. Andy, however, was a natural actor and went on to develop an awesome career in TV shows and commercials. He also became Omar's first dog to be chosen for a proper movie role.

Between them, those two Jacks really took the biscuit.

Andy finally left us at the age of 16 (an impressive 112 in human years) after what had been an amazing life. Tragically, Extreme Pete died much younger, when his curiosity got the better of him and he bit a poisonous toad, whose toxins are lethal to dogs.

I always believed that, once reunited, Pete and Andy were destined to spend eternity frolicking in the big dog run in the sky.

That still doesn't stop me and Omar missing their furry faces, though.

## IF A DOG JUMPS INTO YOUR LAP IT IS BECAUSE HE IS FOND OF YOU, BUT IF A CAT DOES THE SAME THING IT IS BECAUSE YOUR LAP IS WARMER.
*Alfred North Whitehead*

I'm not proud of killing a cat. Now, if it had been a squirrel or a zebra, then that would be something to brag about. But when I moved in with Omar, I also shared my home with some cat-sisters, and I came to the conclusion that they were okay.

Sure, they're sly as can be and nearly always retain an essence of their untamed wildness. They not only slaughter birds, mice, and any defenceless creature they can get their claws on, they torture them for ages first, batting them with their paws to see how long they can survive without an ear or a leg or an eye.

Pick on someone your own size!

And how come most humans (in my experience essentially kind and compassionate beings) repeatedly overlook this daily savagery happening right under their warm, dry noses? Even

Gizmo, one of the few cats I tolerated in my living space (and the smartest I knew), frequently succumbed to his instinctual lust for blood-letting – much to Mercy and Terry's horror. It isn't a coincidence that the word 'feline' is synonymous with furtive, enigmatic, cagey, and sneaky, in my opinion.

Premeditated carnage aside, cats have something about them that I can't help but admire. Apart from the fact that they supposedly have nine lives – now where's the fairness in that? – they meet humans in the middle and entirely on their own terms. With their vindictive ways and sideways glances, they have little of our canine guilelessness or solicitude.

Cats are cruel, but they are also the epitome of cool. They are like a cross between James Dean and Grace Kelly; Daniel Craig and Ingrid Bergman.

I could go on.

'Cat-Gate', as it became known, happened when I was just a few months old and hadn't really figured out that I was a dog yet. All I knew was that, in the spaces between when I wasn't sleeping, eating, or relieving myself, there was so much pent-up energy building inside my little body, I felt as if I was going to explode.

From the moment I grew into my sense of smell, aromas assailed me from all sides. They jammed my olfactory switch-board and urged me to check them out. My chief purpose became to get out of the house, cage, or car I was confined to, escape into the yard, park, or street, and run as fast as I could in any one direction towards the most interesting whiff.

I'd bolt the moment I could to bark and snap at anything that filled my snout, caught my eye, or got in my way. This might include rolling wheels, pigeons, empty plastic bags, squirrels, other dogs, and, occasionally, cats.

Behind those puppy-dog eyes lurked a killer.

My whole body alive with excitement, I'd unleash the powerful forces within me and hurtle through space like a rocket. My fuel was premium-quality puppy pep, my navigation system guided entirely by scent. A kind of mad-dog mist would descend over me, which prevented me from seeing anything clearly or hearing any human cries hurled in my direction. I was, in that moment, beyond help – an accident waiting to happen.

It was on one such occasion, when I was being shown off at a family barbecue in a neighbouring state, that I fell foul of my own primeval instincts. Struggling free from one of the humans who clamoured to squeeze and kiss me, I half jumped, half fell to the ground and scampered for freedom. Before they could stop me, I was across the yard with a joyful yap, then out on the street (where I gave a passing cyclist something to think about). Then, with my low clearance, I was under a neighbour's hedge.

Adjusting my eyes to the darkness, I lifted my muzzle and inhaled something I'd never smelled before – a nose-wrinkling mix of ammonia and dead fish. Yuk!

With my acute sense of hearing, I heard it before I saw it – a low, rumbling growl followed by a hiss. I saw the whites of its fangs and the battle scars across its nose. Its green slits for eyes were fixed on me as it raised a paw and unsheathed an arsenal of talons.

Before I could bark my surprise, it was upon me, scratching and biting, hissing and clawing at my fur, my face, my eyes. Yelping and crashing deeper into the hedge in my haste to get away I rolled in a mess of beaks and bones – a cat's breakfast – sicked up into a gooey mound.

Double yuk!

The creature took advantage of my momentary disgust and was on me again in an instant. It sank its teeth into the soft folds of skin at my neck, causing me to let out a high-pitched yelp that surprised even me. It didn't bring other dogs running, but it certainly brought the humans from across the road. Their shouts of 'Uggie!' startled the beast, which turned quickly to assess what the danger might be.

Seizing my chance, I lunged at it in the darkness and clamped my jaws down hard on what I hoped was its throat. Tasting blood, I knew I'd hit my mark, so I shook and shook what I held between my teeth with all my terrier rage until, finally, it stopped moving.

Backing up out of the hedge in response to the urgent human calls, I dragged my prize with me – eager to show them how brave I'd been in fending off the vicious thing.

As I came out into the light and looked up at the cluster of humans staring down at me, I sensed that they weren't pleased. Dropping my gift to the ground, I saw, to my amazement, that I hadn't slain the creature that had attacked me in her lair at all, but one of her kittens.

I might have been shown leniency for Cat-Gate if it had been a first offence. But coupled with Poop-Gate, Chew-Gate, Stroller-Gate, Puddle-Gate, and Shoe-Gate, my list of misdemeanours across two states had gained me something of an unwanted reputation. In dog and human terms, I was still a minor, but my humans considered me a hopeless case, with blood on my paws. Even though I cocked my head endearingly and rose up on my haunches to look as adorable as was caninely possible, it was only a matter of time before they'd hand me over to the authorities.

'That dog's out of control!' I heard one of them say. 'If we haven't found anyone crazy enough to take him by the end of the week, he's going to the pound.'

I didn't realise it then, but that was the luckiest day of my life. And 'crazy' Omar von Muller was less than a week away from sharing in my great good fortune.

## ACTING IS NOTHING MORE OR LESS THAN PLAYING. THE IDEA IS TO HUMANISE LIFE.
### *George Eliot*

At first, Omar was too busy with work to take me in, so he asked a female friend to look after me for a week or so. Things began reasonably well, although I was put in the 'slammer' in the back yard for a couple of minor offences.

Events took a turn for the worse when I was publicly insulted by her billy goat, which had a sinister look about it, to my mind. Admittedly, all it did was scrape the ground and flap its rubbery lips at me (with some baring of yellow teeth), but that was enough to get my goat.

Goat-Gate began when I lurched at the beast to voice my indignation. The demon lowered its horns and tried to prod me with one of them. Sensing that there was a game to be had, I ran round and round the creature until it grew dizzy and had no idea which direction I was coming from. Only when it was facing the other way and braying like a donkey did I jump up and sink my little needle teeth into its haunches.

I'd watched a few rodeos on TV, and I always pitied those poor animals when complete strangers jumped on their back and forced them to buck around a ring. I can tell you now, though, that riding the rump of that overgrown kid with little more than a mouthful of wiry hair to hang onto was one of the most exhilarating experiences of my life.

Somewhere in the background, I could hear his owner's increasingly frantic cries. I caught glimpses of her reddened face as she yelled at me and tugged on my tail, urging me to let go, but I wasn't going to yield for anyone or anything.

Yee-ha!

Dispatched to Omar, disgraced, I showed little remorse and quickly checked out my new digs. Omar's comfortable house in North Hollywood was truly a place where dogs were kings

As well as Extreme Pete and Andy (whom I liked immediately), I shared my quarters with three other dogs, including a couple of skittish she-dogs, a brown Jack mutt mix called Brando who'd been rescued from a pound, and a pug she-dog named Chata. We also lived with four pigeons, two cats, and a yellow-headed Amazon parrot called Mango who, to my mind, was evil incarnate.

Soon to join us was Gordo, the son of Omar's prize American bulldog Nikko (who'd won more competition titles than any American bulldog ever). Omar called him Gordo because it meant 'fat' in Spanish. He'd been in a few commercials and low-budget movies, but popped his knee training for a movie called *Beer for My Horses* and needed an operation. Gordo was the brother I'd always longed for, and our friendship was true and lifelong.

Playing roughhouse with my
frat brother Gordo.

My new roomies were predominantly male, and Omar was single back then, so we guys totally ruled the roost. That place was Animal House. Which was just as well, because in my first few hours, I ran around the place like a narcotics hound sniffing everything. I tested the furniture for size and decided on my preferred position – middle of the sofa, opposite the TV – and then I left my mark on the corner of the armchair.

I wasn't allowed to get away with anything, though. Dad Omar was quite strict and expected us to adhere to the house rules, which included no unlawful peeing, pooping, chewing, barking, fighting, or stealing. He was never mean, I was relieved to discover, and he preferred instead to reward good behaviour. The worst that might happen was a sharp jerk on my leash if I was wearing one, or a sudden pinch of my neck. If I'd been really bad, he might grab me firmly either side of my jaw and stare at me eyeball to eyeball. With those intense eyes of his that would make even a beagle give up smoking, he'd let me know in an unusually stern voice who was pack leader.

I can't say that I entirely believed him at first, so I decided to test it out. Needless to say, I fell foul of all five house rules in my first few weeks. Omar kept the evidence for months to prove my guilt.

Exhibit A was a stain on the living-room carpet.

Exhibit B was the needle teeth marks on the legs of his revolving office chair.

Exhibit C was the scar on the nose of Gordo (which I felt added to his suitability for attack roles).

Finally, Exhibit D was the dent in the bars of Mango's cage.

My worst misdemeanour was tipping over the trash can to rummage through the contents on the kitchen floor at my leisure. This was a habit I'd learned early in my first house and found almost impossible to quit.

'I guess this proves you're food-motivated, at least,' Omar told me with a sigh on the fifth occasion he came home to find me in the middle of the linoleum chewing on a pizza carton. 'But this isn't how we do things round here.'

Olfactory entertainment,
Jack Russell style.

Picked up by the scruff of my neck, I was hoisted outside and placed into a new 'slammer' – a small outdoor kennel with a caged run and only water to drink. This separation from the rest of my pack did not please me, and I yelped my puppy indignation. Omar stood firm, though, and after a while my periods in what came to be known as 'Sing Sing' (for all the noise I made in it) lessened week by week – if only out of consideration for the neighbours.

He did have to buy an Uggie-proof trash can though, just in case of a relapse.

## DOGS ARE MIRACLES WITH PAWS.
### *Unknown*

Once I'd picked up the basics of life in the all-singing, all-dancing Von Muller family, Dad officially enrolled me in his acting school, in the hope that he could channel some of my juvenile exuberance into comic drama.

Not that he had any such pretensions, but he was following in the footprints of some of the great coaches of all time, such as Constantin Stanislavski (founder of Method acting), Lee Strasberg, Sanford Meisner, and Stella Adler – who taught Brando, Garland, and De Niro, among many others.

Miss Adler especially would have been proud of the work Omar did with me, because one of her maxims was 'Don't be boring', and he made sure I was never, ever that.

He began with some basic obedience coaching; a process that can take up to a year. Mostly it involved a lot of hand signals accompanied by basic prompts, both of which would be repeated over and over again. By shaking a hand at me containing some sort of sausage or dried liver treat, he began to teach me right from wrong, as well as how to control my basic animal urges. In this easy-to-learn system of rewards, my greed helped me learn my new cues quickly. Pizza had become one of my all-time favourite foods (thanks to leftovers in the trash can), but Dad insisted it wasn't good for me, so I had to make do with something healthier – usually mini hotdogs in pork, chicken, or vegetable flavours.

Taking acting lessons
from my coach Omar.

In addition to speaking Spanish and English, Omar created an extraordinary sequence of sounds with his mouth that included clicking and high-pitched animal noises. He also used squeaky toys, which never failed to grab my attention (my favourite was Stinky the skunk, which I played with until it fell apart). I had never known a human with such infinite patience, who so rarely chastised me for my mistakes. I adored every minute of my one-to-one time with him, especially when it ended with a treat.

In this mutually beneficial environment, he and I began to develop as perfect an understanding as there can be between two living beings. There felt to me to be something almost mystical about our connection. I knew from my favourite astrology channel on TV (which Omar left on when he wasn't playing soft jazz to keep us calm) that Aquarians who team up with fellow Aquarians share a love of adventurousness, while still admiring each other's individuality.

That's exactly how it was with us.

He always said I was one of his fastest learners, and I certainly kept my big brown eyes glued to him at all times, and my pert little ears cocked and ready for my next cue. Within a matter of days, I had learnt the basic stage directions of 'Sit', 'Down', 'Come', and – the most important of all – 'Stay'. Within weeks, I'd come along leaps and bounds and acquired 'Roll Over', 'Sit-Stay', 'Down-Stay', 'Walk', 'Turn Around', and 'Bow'.

I learned how to use my mouth to pick up and fetch things or bite for a ball through the pants of somebody without injuring them. Omar taught me how to use my vocal instrument to the best of my ability with a shake of his hand or the single cue of 'Speak'.

I could scratch frenziedly at a door and sit up on my back legs for several minutes at a time. I could walk slowly on the cue of 'Slow' and creep along the ground on my belly. I was able to leap up and kick someone in the guts, or jump through hoops, including those Omar made with his arms. I'd grip something with my teeth and not let go until told, even if lifted off the floor and swung round and round (great fun!).

The word 'Bang!' made me roll over dead and stay there until told to get up. 'Go With' meant follow him or someone else. 'Stay With' meant stay with that person, even if there were major distractions like a car, smoke, mysterious smells, or sudden loud noises.

We both sensed that I was a natural from the start. I so loved my coaching sessions that I would always be despondent when they were over. Soaking up Omar's every word like a sponge, I increased my vocabulary enormously and soon got to grips with some of his more exotic phrases like 'amigo', 'padre', and 'bueno'.

Little did I know how multilingual I was to become.

For any aspiring canine actors out there, I am living proof that there is no substitute for work, work, and more work. You can be as smart as you like, with a fine intellect and a keen sense of how to register emotions, but unless you pay attention and respond swiftly to the cues you're given, then you are doomed to be a lowly extra.

As Omar explained later: 'Not only was Uggie extremely photogenic, but he had an amazing natural energy. He quickly became known for his sense of humour; he made everyone laugh and liked to control the situation. He was hugely popular wherever I took him.'

Dad always said that one of my greatest gifts was that I was fearless. That wasn't strictly correct, as I was secretly terrified of losing him. My apparent lack of fear, I can now reveal here, exclusively, came through the trust we had in each other. Having learned and accepted the premise of my most important cues, I decided to follow them to the letter with mute acceptance. I grew to believe that Omar wouldn't allow anyone to hurt me – not him, not a child, a stranger, a director, or any member of a cast or crew.

My new Dad had my best interests at heart.

Trust was the true secret of my craft.

**8**

## THE WORLD WAS CONQUERED
## THROUGH THE UNDERSTANDING OF
## DOGS; THE WORLD EXISTS THROUGH
## THE UNDERSTANDING OF DOGS.
*Friedrich Nietzsche*

Not that I knew much about trust from the beginning. Back then, it was just a complete doggy love-fest. The feelings I developed for Omar were intense and lifelong. I might have wavered off my path a little in my youth, but I'd found my way home.

Omar was my True North.

To my delight, I did so well in my coaching sessions that I became a fully enlisted member of the Von Muller troupe. That meant I was allowed to join the other dogs whenever Omar took them to street parties, or to the Third Street Promenade in Santa Monica to entertain the public for biscuit money and laughs. It was a way of getting us accustomed to crowds and noise and to show off some of our many talents.

Omar had started out performing on the streets of Venice Beach, but was soon moved along by the authorities because of the leash law (as if we needed to be on leashes!). It was the best thing that could have happened to us, because in Santa Monica there was an even more appreciative crowd. As well as enjoying every minute of our show, we were adding to our training and experience every time we went.

Every actor has to start somewhere,
even as a stand-up comic.

Eight-year-old Andy was the star back then, skilled at agility stunts and jumping through a hoop like a pro, while the rest of us sat waiting our turn in a row on a bench. Brando was another great skateboarder and the undisputed clown. Even Gizmo the cat came along. He could give Omar a few high-fives and his speciality was standing up on his back legs and looking like he was boxing. Poor Pete was still too shy to be around crowds, so he was left behind.

Initially, I sat on the bench, sniffing the wind. The smell of hot dogs and hamburgers, coffee and popcorn switched on my drool tap every time. To keep me from obsessing about food, Omar enlisted me to help run the box office. It became my job to accept the dollar bills offered to me by members of the audience, in appreciation of Andy's antics, and then leap through a hoop and drop the money in a bucket with a little bow. I loved all the fuss and frequently licked any hand that offered me cash. Like all aspiring actors, though, I began to tire of the repetitive nature of my work and longed for a bigger role. Surely the biz we call 'show' was my true destiny?

Besides, dollar bills are not delicious, and more than once I punished them by shredding them to pieces as Omar yelled, 'Uggie! No!'

My antics worked, because he picked up on my eagerness to do more and set about coaching me to take a bigger part. Before long, I was not only jumping through hoops, but leaping great divides between ramps like a furry Evel Knievel. I also learned to improvise whenever one of my canine buddies made a mistake. Brando, especially, was a sloppy dollar dropper, so whenever he missed the bucket, I'd jump off my bench, quick as a flash, and pick it up for him with a little bow, which always got more laughs (and often tips).

With the eyes of the crowd upon me, I milked the applause like a pro. On more than one occasion, I was handed a $50 note, and one day someone gave me a $100 bill.

Needless to say, I didn't shred that one.

Even better than the tips, Omar was approached by dozens of owners who so loved what they saw that they wanted him to train their unruly mutts. 'I'd like my dog to come when I call, for starters,' they might say, adding, 'and if you can teach him to skateboard, too, that'd be really cool!'

As if it was something you could learn in a few days!

Dad also had offers of studio work for Andy, and even Gizmo got a gig – a sleep-on, lick-on part in the Tom Petty video 'Swingin''. So, as well as all the fun we had, we might pick up a $3,000 training job or an even more lucrative deal for a commercial. And they called this work?

I have to admit that the job was a lot tougher for Omar than it ever was for me. Over the years, he was given some really difficult dogs to train; the mastiffs, bulldogs, and mixed breeds that nobody else would touch. If their training didn't work out, he knew that they would most likely end up being euthanised. Bearing that in mind, he always went the extra mile. So much so that a friend of his spent her spare time rescuing dogs from Doggy Death Row and taking them to Omar to socialise them.

One such dog was a small, black puggle. 'Nobody can handle this dog,' the sweet-scented lady friend told Dad. 'She's off-the-wall crazy; probably because pugs and poodles shouldn't be mixed.'

Omar brought the vicious little puggle home, and we took one look at her glazed, terrified eyes and kept well away. After several weeks, he finally managed to calm her down enough to accept a leash and go out with him in public. No matter how much progress he made with her, though, something would always freak her out.

A sudden movement or noise would make that little live wire scream like a banshee. She'd snap and snarl, then poop everywhere. She'd cower and literally try to climb the walls if Omar or any of us went near her. He'd go back to the beginning, but she'd soon lose it again. There was something seriously wrong with her. She'd roll her eyes back in her head and that would be it – her mind would go to Planet Puggle.

One day, she interpreted something Omar did as a threat, and she jumped up and bit him badly on his face, close to his eye. He bled and bled and could have lost his sight. Reluctantly, he rang his friend and told her that this was the first animal for which he was going to have to admit defeat.

'No one can ever adopt this one,' he said. 'She could really hurt someone. It wouldn't be responsible.' The friend was so upset that she couldn't bear to take the demented pooch to the vet to end her suffering, so Omar did. It broke his heart too, but it was probably one of the kindest things he ever did.

Undaunted, the friend brought Omar another dog – this time a wild hound that had been captured in the hills above

Pasadena. There was a pack of them up there that had started stealing from trash cans and become such a nuisance that people were shooting or poisoning them. The trouble was, this animal had never been close to a human in her life. If Omar even went near her, she would drop down and lie totally flat on the ground.

Out in the dog run, she'd sleep all day and only walk around at night, as had been the nocturnal pattern of her pack. Having watched her behaviour for a few days, Dad began by taking her for a walk at night, literally dragging her around on a leash to start with. It took three months of intensive training and socialisation but, incredibly, that dog was adopted by a man who'd never owned a pet before. To everyone's surprise and delight, the once wild pack animal ended up living with him in mutual bliss in the metropolis of New York City, of all places.

One of Omar's other great success stories was with a ten-year-old German shepherd that was so devoted to its elderly owner that it wouldn't allow anyone near him. As the man grew more infirm and needed nursing care, this became a major problem. You can't teach an old dog new tricks – or so the saying goes – but Omar proved everyone wrong. Even though that German shepherd had him pinned to the ground on one of their first outings in the park (after he tripped and the dog misinterpreted his actions), he soon had it eating out of his hand – literally.

'The day I fell, the dog stood on my chest, snarling and dripping drool on my face,' he said. 'I really thought that might be the end of me, but I just turned my head away until he climbed down and walked off. I began his obedience training right away, and three days later, I could place my entire hand inside his mouth without any threat of injury. He just needed someone to tell him, "No".'

Dad had long believed that the secret to successful animal training was teaching boundaries and respect. 'You see some celebrity trainers talking about how an owner has to make himself the dominant wolf in the pack by never allowing a dog on a bed and that kind of thing, but that's not true. You can sleep with a dog and pamper it, if you have first taught them right from wrong. The discipline has to be absolute, but also tempered with kindness.'

He frequently complained that nobody on TV is ever shown yanking hard on the leash, or grabbing an animal by the neck, because they're afraid it might look bad. 'I love my dogs like children,' Omar said, 'but you have to be tough on them right from the start, so they know who's boss. Once they get that, you can spoil them all you like.'

As a one-time convicted felon turned international movie star, I am living proof that his methods work.

## FIND IN YOURSELF THOSE HUMAN
## THINGS WHICH ARE UNIVERSAL.
### *Sanford Meisner*

Having taught me my boundaries and trained me for street theatre, Omar could tell I was ready for bigger things. He decided to teach me how to skateboard and tackle some of the more extreme sports. Andy was getting older, and Pete still couldn't face crowds, whereas I'd always lapped up the attention.

As he said later, 'Uggie was a born actor. I always knew he was capable of so much more.' Coaching a dog to skateboard takes a lot longer than any of the basics we'd gone through before, however, and there were times when I considered giving up and just lying around watching TV with Gordo.

Omar began by feeding me all my meals from his hands, and only his hands. 'Good dog, Uggs,' he'd say, as I chomped on some chicken or pieces of sausage. 'There's a good *muchacho.*'

Then he got me the right tool for the job: a skateboard that was perfect for my height, weight, and bone structure. It had to be light, strong, and smooth to ride. 'I always go top of the line on wheels, trucks, ball bearings, and boards,' he explained, as he adapted the board to suit me. 'I think it makes a big difference.' He trimmed away the edges which he assured me might get in my way and make it difficult for someone starting out.

He picked a spot in the front yard for us to start our coaching – a small patch of grass by the sidewalk. We only ever trained in the cool of the mornings or evenings, so that I didn't get too hot. He set the board on the grass, so it wouldn't roll. He also locked the wheels, and began by teaching me to jump on and off the board as if it were a low table. I was hand-fed on that rock-solid board every day for weeks, and praised warmly every time I stepped up onto it. Eventually, I felt 100 per cent confident and comfortable.

Next, he made me do some obedience exercises on the board, including 'Sit', 'Down', 'Stay', and 'Turn Around'. Once I'd mastered that, he began to move it slowly from side to side when I was on it, shaking it a little or lifting it off the ground, but making sure I didn't get scared. Every instinct in my wiry little body told me to jump off that moving plank, so on the few occasions I did, Omar went back a step or two, until I figured out that it was safe.

He took his time. We'd train for maybe 10 minutes at a stretch and then he'd put the board away, to my crushing disappointment. When he brought it out again the following day, my tail wagged like a metronome.

Once he felt that nothing would faze me, he loosened the wheels a little and put the board on the sidewalk. Then he began to roll it along with me on it, with the promise of a treat if I stayed on. After a while, he attached a nylon rope to the front and pulled me along slowly, always stopping it with his foot if it went too fast or I seemed unsure.

Repetition, diligence, patience, and positive reinforcement were the keys to success. It was the last part I loved the best. 'Awesome, Uggie!' Dad might say as he slipped me a bacon bit, or 'Good job!' or 'That a boy!' with a liver treat. In no time at all, he was able to pull me around the block.

I'd experienced some public admiration at our street performances in the past (although never as much as the skateboarding superstars). The attention I began to attract as a cute Jack Russell riding a skateboard, however, really went to my furry head. The motivation to do more, go faster, be better was overpowering. Before I knew it, I was clinging to that deck with all four paws, as Omar loosened the wheels some more and let me pick up speed to lead me down hills and up kerbs.

Instinctively I'd contract my muscles and lean into a curve. Or I might put out a rear paw to steady myself or push the board along. Before I knew it, there was no nylon rope anymore; it was just me – free and easy, with the California breeze flapping my ears – following Omar across an empty parking lot. Within weeks, I could steer and do entire routines. In my red bandana, I'd kick off against the sidewalk. After maybe a hundred hours of coaching, I was bumping down stairs and shredding ramps.

I picked up some of the terminology from my fellow (human) skateboarders and learned to 'ollie' off the kickers or 'grind' a ledge, my mouth open, catching air. I was stoked.

The high was so addictive that I forgot about the treats that had once been my sole motivation. Now I understood why Pete had been so hooked. Omar used to have to pull the skateboard away from Pete, or he'd have kept going until he expired from exhaustion and heat.

Being on that board was reward enough.

I had never felt more human in my life.

## ACTING IS A FORM
## OF CONFESSION.
### *Tallulah Bankhead*

Things had been going well, and Omar was so impressed with my progress that he decided to enter me in a TV show called *Pet Star* on the Animal Planet channel.

Gordo and I had watched it with him dozens of times. Humans took their animals to compete in front of celebrity judges in the hope that their tricks would earn them the most points. The $25,000 final prize ensured that standards were high. Dogs featured heavily, and Omar once took Brando all the way to the final with his skateboarding skills, but – although he won $2,000 – he was pipped at the post by the show's first major winner, an Australian blue cattle dog named Skidboot, who belonged to a Texan farmer.

Darn, that dog was good. He knew the difference between right and left, could turn on a dime, give a high-five, and appeared to be able to count. Skidboot could balance a biscuit on his nose and just sit without trying to eat it. I wasn't sure I could exercise the same restraint.

Omar wasn't fazed. 'Uggie can skateboard, walk backwards, play dead, bow, and do all kinds of other stuff,' he told his sweet-smelling new girlfriend, Mercy, who'd recently come into our lives. 'He'll breeze through the auditions.'

We got to the live show presented by Mario Lopez, and all was going well. That was, until we stood in the wings, waiting to go on. To Omar's dismay (and my delight), the contestant immediately before us was a white cockatoo, which was perched on the arm of its unsuspecting human.

Now, parrots and I had some history. From the day I set paw inside Omar's house, Mango definitely had it in for me. It was as if he were saying, 'Not another flea-bitten dog!' Mango didn't like Omar much, either – in fact, he hated all males and only had eyes for the ladies but he especially disliked terriers for some reason. He'd squawk furiously or repeat Omar's cues in that grating high-pitched voice of his. 'Ug-geee Stay! Ug-gee Sit!' He'd fluff his feathers and throw seed husks at me, or flap his wings and spray me with his drinking water.

I took a dislike to that overgrown budgie and did my best to jump up and snap at him, but his cage was too far out of my reach. Only once, when he was released to fly around, did I get near enough to close my mouth around his scrawny body, but he wriggled free. I was spitting out a couple of his green tail feathers while he circled above, bombing me with poop. Jumping up again, I knocked over his cage and dented it. That pesky Polly shrieked and flapped so much, his protests must have been heard five blocks away.

My hackles were up similarly as soon as I saw the cockatoo at my *Pet Star* debut. The unsuspecting owner balanced it on a perch, right near where Omar and I were waiting to go on, before he ran out onto the stage to announce himself and summon the bird. At that point, I barked and lunged at the cockatoo, causing him to take off prematurely and zigzag across the set erratically. Instead of getting on with his act, the owner spent the next few minutes trying to catch the parrot and calm it down enough to do its stupid bird tricks, which, as I recall, involved little more than a bell and a ball.

'Bad boy!' Omar chastised me, and he made me sit and stay. But I couldn't take my eyes off that parrot, which was still extremely ruffled by my presence.

When it had finally been carried off stage right, in disgrace, and it was our turn to go on, I was still shaking with excitement at the thought of that feather-ball mocking me, without the protection of any cage. I managed to focus just enough to perform most of my routine, but with my snout to the ceiling and my eyes scanning the curtains for a glimmer of white feather, I was never really going to impress. I stepped off the skateboard and stood quivering when I thought I glimpsed a wing in the wings, and I broke into wild barking at the parrot's unhappy human. Omar could do little but apologise as we made a hasty exit.

Cockatoo-Gate was soon followed by Mud-Gate, when I dug a huge hole in the flowerbed (careful to avoid my favourite bush). It was mostly a reflex thing; I was a terrier after all – bred to dig into the earths of foxes and flush them out. The blood of my wild ancestors still coursed through my veins, and I was merely responding to ancient instincts.

Well, that was my excuse anyway.

In truth, Mud-Gate was also a protest at being kept outside one afternoon. When it rained, I rolled in the wet dirt until I was completely covered. I heard Omar return home, so I scratched at the back door to be let in, but for a few minutes he had no idea which of his dogs I was. Only by a process of elimination did he figure it out.

My so-called 'punishment'? A warm bath with lemon-scented shampoo, followed by a brisk rub down with a towel (always a treat for a Jack).

## A LOVER TRIES TO STAND IN WELL WITH
## THE PET DOG OF THE HOUSE.
### *Molière*

I hadn't had many female influences in my life since my milky, pre-weaning days. My first lady human never had much time for me, it seemed. Omar was single, and way too busy for any kind of social life, so Chata, the pug, became the she-dog for me.

Chata was a vision in fur. From the moment I saw her magnificent curves, I thought, 'Bow-wow!' Much older than me at six (42 in human years), she had such a scrunchy face that I hardly noticed the age difference at all. I mean, what's another wrinkle when you're a pug?

Chata smelled wonderful; truly alluring, and in all the right places. I wanted to slobber all over that button-eyed babe the minute I saw her – and I mean all over – which is pretty much what I did. She was so sweet-natured that she didn't mind me nibbling her ears or sniffing her backside at all; sometimes she even did it back to me, which was bliss.

Dear Chata was the exception to the rule in the Von Muller troupe, in that she had virtually no bankable talent at all. Her little legs were too short to skateboard. Her breathing was laboured which meant she snorted all the time, and she could barely keep up with the rest of us. She snored even louder than I did, and that was saying something. But to me, she was a queen.

Which is not to say she hadn't overcome adversity. Chata was a rescue dog, like me. Omar had been a sucker for pooches in peril since he was a lad, and he could rarely resist a sob story (it was one of the qualities I admired most in him and hoped to emulate one day). He'd rescued a couple of other she-dogs, too, including a wheaten terrier called Lacy and a terrier mix named Loca. Both were easy to train, and Lacy was especially talented at playing dead – so much so that her limbs could be manipulated and she could even be held aloft in mid-air. But they were both too fearful of noise to work in show business, which is when Omar decided to work only with he-dogs.

Wise choice, if I do say so myself.

The movie industry had a long and respected history of using rescue hounds in films, right back to the days of Rin Tin Tin. Charlie Chaplin saved a piebald mongrel from a pound to play the endearing stray 'Scraps' in his 1918 classic *A Dog's Life*. Higgins, the dog who played Benji, was saved from an animal shelter, too, as was Spike, who played the title lead in *Old Yeller* (surely the saddest movie ever made).

The American Humane Association estimated that approximately 80 per cent of the cats and dogs seen on TV and in movies were rescued and/or adopted, which often surprises humans – but from where else could an actor draw on his angst?

Sadly for me, my beloved Chata had her eyes set on a rescue dog other than me. Hurricane Andy had just finished his first leading role in a motion picture – the 2002 Jack Black comedy *Orange County*, and I'm afraid Chata, when it came to movie stars, was more tramp than lady.

Her black eyes followed Andy everywhere he went. Her stump of a tail wagged if he even glanced in her direction. She diligently licked his bowl clean once he'd finished. Shameless, she'd roll over in front of him and flaunt her feminine form at him. Extreme Pete was always happy to ogle her, but Andy was the best. He knew how I felt about the pug, so he kept his distance. That only seemed to make the lovesick Chata worship him more. I had to find someone else to adore.

Mercy was the last kind of she-dog I was looking for. Apart from the fact that she was human, she was pointedly Omar's mate. A friend of his grown-up daughter from his first family, she worked in a law office with her in Miami when a match was suggested. From the moment he set those puppy-dog eyes on her, Omar seemed as lovesick as Chata.

Jeez. All that drooling over a human?

Puh-leeze!

Another thing about Mercy was that she had, to my mind, way too much hair. Her lustrous black tresses would surely present moulting issues.

Mercy was also a neat freak, and – even though she hadn't been granted full house privileges in the early days – she took it upon herself to clean up our crazy bachelor pad. Out went the dirty laundry and unwashed bowls that had long provided us with so much olfactory stimulation. In came a battery of solvents and pungent-smelling cleaning fluids that stung the nose and made our eyes water.

With my Cuban long-coat
Mom, Mercy.

My greatest concern was that Mercy might become my chief rival for Dad's affection, and I was soon proved right. Annoyingly, he spent more time kissing and cuddling her than he did me. I growled menacingly at her a few times to assert my position as the alpha male, but she just patted my head and laughed. It wasn't exactly the display of submission I'd hoped for. In the end, we agreed to tolerate each other, on the grounds that we both loved Omar.

I had grown so well accustomed to sleeping on Dad's bed with four other dogs that my other fear was that the arrival of Mercy in our pack would mean an unseemly jockeying for position. I needn't have fretted. While the leggy Cuban long-coat didn't curl up on the floor (as I might have expected of a new arrival), she did seem to respect my status in the family ranking, so I decided to make room for her.

Occasionally, I'd be kicked off the super-king, but I was always allowed back on after she and Dad had finished what seemed to be an unnecessarily frequent amount of mutual grooming.

'We're getting married, guys!' Omar announced one day in 2004 out of the blue, his eyes showing his happiness. 'You're all gonna have a Mom!'

We sensed his excitement and jumped up to bark, wag our tails, and show our general appreciation (apart from Gizmo). But we were disappointed to learn that all this meant was a spell in the kennels, while they went down to the courthouse and then off to the Napa Valley for their honeymoon.

In the blink of an eye (well, 10 months later), Mercy's belly swelled out of all proportion, and out popped a baby human they named Terry. I prided myself on having my paw on the pulse, but events were moving way too fast for my liking!

What I didn't expect in the great scheme of my life, though, was how deeply I would come to care for my new little 'sister'. I had seen, with Omar and Mercy, how magnificently humans loved, and I guessed some of that outpouring of emotion must have rubbed off on me. I was suddenly feeling more affection than I ever thought caninely possible.

Giving some puppy love to
my 'sister' Terry.

It shouldn't have been that surprising, as I was slowly coming to the conclusion that the only difference between Omar and me was that he had two fewer legs and opposable thumbs.

Mom and Dad doted on their new baby girl, who, as a bawling bundle of poop and vomit, should – by all the dogs in heaven – have repulsed me. Instead, Terry crawled her way into my terrier heart and staked a lifelong claim. Sensing her infant vulnerability, I became extremely protective of her and watched her master every faltering step.

**12**

## THE DOG WAS CREATED SPECIALLY FOR
## CHILDREN. HE IS A GOD OF FROLIC.
*Henry Ward Beecher*

One of the qualities I most admired in Omar was his enormous capacity for forgiveness. No matter how badly I'd behaved in the past, or how long it took me to master a new talent, he seemed able to overlook my weaknesses and focus on my strengths.

I am relieved and delighted to say that he was right to believe in me. Under his tutelage and within relatively few dog years, I became utterly dedicated to my craft. Not only could I skateboard almost as well as the late, great Pete, I also learned how to walk on my back legs for extended periods and became a master at pretending to be shot by an imaginary gun.

When I took up water-skiing, though, I discovered a whole new passion. Dad came up with the idea when he saw how confident Brando, Pete, and I were on a skateboard. He took us to a creek and tried us on a small surf board that he dragged back and forth through the water. We not only kept our balance, even in a current, we wagged our tails madly throughout, to show our appreciation of this new game.

As Omar said afterwards, 'They took to it right away. I couldn't believe it. If they fell off, they'd scramble straight back on to have some more fun. I think they enjoyed it even more than skateboarding.'

He bought a Jet Ski to use on a lake near our home and started taking us out most weekends and towing us along behind him. People loved to watch what Dad referred to as his 'little guys' riding the surf. Brando loved it so much; he stood up on that board like a miniature lion to roar at the waves.

I'd never had so much fun in my life. Man, what a thrill it was to feel the wind and the spray in my face! Every sinew in my body strained to maximise the sensation, as I leaned into the surf. If I could have been fed a sausage or two while water-skiing, I think I might have actually died and gone to dog heaven.

Best of all, Omar discovered that while a talented dog such as Jumpy (who'd been bought for $50 from a kid who told him his father was going to put the dog down) might have many more 'behaviours' in his repertoire than me, I was the one who could milk a crowd. On or off the water, most days, I acted circles around the rest of the animals – especially lazy Gizmo the cat, who just had to sit around, sleep, or look inquisitive during most of his professional engagements.

I mean, how demanding was that?

And so it was that, in spite of Cockatoo-Gate and Goat-Gate (plus a few mini-Gates inbetween), Dad still believed in me. He signed me up with some animal talent agencies and offered my services for TV, commercials, and print campaigns. We were ready. He'd helped me enough with my character work and advised me as best he could.

**Leaning into the surf, the spray in my face.**

It was time to go pro.

'You have star potential, buddy,' he told me as part of my positive reinforcement coaching. 'Trust me, you could go all the way.'

And this from a human who'd trained Jumpy to leap 12 feet high, paint with his teeth, walk on his front legs, challenge the world balloon-popping record, and wink on demand.

With my newfound maturity, at the ripe old age of 14 in dog years, I saw how well the other members of the troupe performed and sensed that Omar would be mightily disappointed if I let him down. It was time to put away puppyish things: relinquish my squeaky skunk, stop chasing Mango, give up messing about in trash cans, and knuckle down to business.

He sent my photograph in to various modelling agencies and talent scouts, and the work slowly started to trickle in. I was quickly picked for a couple of print campaigns and cast for a supermarket commercial, but the industry was tougher than I thought. We had been wise not to give up my daytime boulevard business.

Typecasting was an issue I hadn't prepared myself for, especially when – to my mind – I possessed such range. With one glance at my portfolio, though, it seemed the powers that be would immediately assume that, although photogenic, I was either a) naughty or b) smart, with not much inbetween.

I longed to show them how gallant and heroic I could be, along with cute, fierce, frightened, hungry, despairing, and gleeful.

Still, every job was different, and I enjoyed the variety. We'd usually arrive early on set or at a photographic studio, and Omar would introduce me to the crew and acclimatise me to the environment. I'd trot around confidently, sniffing each of the staff in turn, and being sure to show them only my most endearing qualities.

It would be Dad's job to make sure that the temperature was ambient – neither too hot nor too cold – and check that there was a fresh water supply and somewhere for me to pee and poop. Hair and make-up would often take some time, depending on the requirements. If I needed to be 'touched in', or even a different colour, then a make-up artist would be brought in to use natural vegetable dyes to make me look the part.

Most people didn't appreciate the extraordinary amount of effort that went into each shot in a shoot or commercial. Omar would be fully versed in the storyboard or script, so that we would know what was to be expected of me. We'd have rehearsed my scene over and over at home, or in a studio if necessary, until we had it off pat. Hour upon hour was wasted as the human models and actors sorted themselves out and tried to iron out their mistakes. If only they'd watch and learn from a canine master.

Nothing was left to chance, and Omar was very careful to make sure that I was always calm, comfortable, and safe. He earned every morsel of whatever his percentage was … probably 15 per cent of the sausages? I'm not really interested in the business side.

I admit that some of my earliest work may have lacked the finesse of my later roles, but it did have a raw charm that endeared me to my growing army of fans. Cutting my acting teeth in commercials allowed me to develop my talents.

Whenever I was selected to advertise pet food, household appliances, or cars, I did my best to get inside the mind-set of the director, so that I could really give him what he wanted.

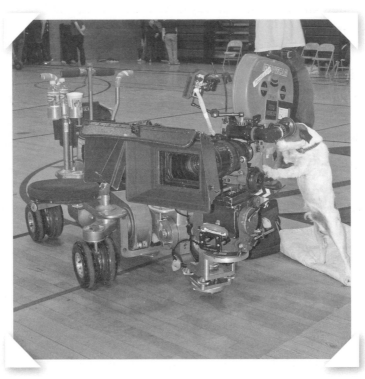

**Checking that the camera will capture my best angle.**

For a TV commercial for a new range of central-heating boilers, for example, I was asked to jump up out of my dog bed and watch, head cocked, as one wild animal after another broke in through the flap in the back door to sneak inside and keep warm.

'Uggie must look surprised and maybe a little perturbed by the new arrivals, but he mustn't attack them,' the director insisted.

I could tell Dad was nervous as the director presented him with a list of creatures I'd be faced with: rabbits, a raccoon, a fox, a corgi, and a skunk (I kid you not). Wisely, he'd recently put a 'no parrot' clause into my contract. He stood immediately behind the camera to keep eye contact with me as best he could. I sat on my mark and did exactly as was expected of me, fighting all my natural instincts and stopping myself from going mad-dog when a brainless bunny bumped straight into me on my final, all-important shot.

I did several e-cards for American Greetings, including one that also featured Guido and two other dogs. It was entitled 'Woofy Birthday', in which we all barked the 'Happy Birthday' song. In one of my favourite e-cards, for Christmas, I was depicted as a lone pup in a snowy back yard, my kennel festooned with fairy lights. First I had to emerge with a fur-trimmed stocking, and then hang it on a hook. It was tricky, but I mastered it.

Then I had to push a plate of cookies out into the snow and leave them, which called on all my self-control. Nudging a full pint of milk next to the plate was a messy business and took several takes. Omar ended up using a special little track on which the glass could be rolled along and smeared baby food on it to entice me to nudge it further. With much practice, I finally managed it.

Wandering further into the yard, I had to rise up on my haunches and bark my Christmas wish list to Santa before going back to my kennel to settle down and wait next to the scrummy-smelling cookies. After turning round and round a few times and checking the starry sky, I was finally allowed to grab one of the cookies, which I wolfed down quickly, in case the director changed his mind.

Stupidly, I didn't fluff that part, or we'd have had to go again. I might even have bolted three cookies – I mean takes – out of it.

In the final scene, lying on the ground by the kennel, I had to pretend to be asleep (not a stretch for me), as Santa's gloved hand appeared and placed a large bone wrapped in ribbon on the ground next to me – before stealing one of my cookies! Then the words scrolled up: 'May all your Christmas wishes come true.'

Adorable, huh?

**13**

## ALL KNOWLEDGE, THE TOTALITY OF ALL QUESTIONS AND ALL ANSWERS IS CONTAINED IN THE DOG.
### *Franz Kafka*

With a growing reputation as a potential star who could perform most of my scenes in a single take, I'd never been busier. Coupled with my modelling schedule, it was vital that I remained in tip-top condition.

At 16 pounds, it was said that I weighed slightly more than the average Hollywood actress. I don't know about that, but I do know that most starlets couldn't have kept up with my punishing regime.

Omar was careful to make sure that I didn't gain too much weight or lose stamina by sitting around the set all day. He'd take me for short walks or play games with me to relieve the boredom, but we could never stray too far from the set. There were inevitably delays as one human after another screwed up, and everyone would have to go again.

On a rare afternoon off, I slouched on the couch with Gordo and watched a TV programme about Frank Sinatra, in which he claimed that he got out of making movies because the waiting drove him crazy. He became known as 'one-shot Sinatra' and believed that everyone should be as well prepared as he was, ready for a single take.

Smooth criminal? My Michael
Jackson impression.

I'm with you, Mr S!

Exercise and diet are key in my business, and so it was with professional zeal that I devoted myself to Frisbee, flyball, and chasing birds and squirrels for general fitness. On weekends, there was always skateboarding and water-skiing to burn off a few extra calories. To cool down, I'd commit myself to at least twenty minutes of deep breathing and then some stretching – or as I liked to call it, 'doga'. As often as I could, I'd get a little sun on the beach.

Omar is extraordinarily well versed in nutrition, and he fed me mainly raw chicken or beef, which he ground up in a mincer – bones and all! He'd add broccoli or cauliflower for extra vitamins. He began that regime after taking advice from animal nutritionists and being alarmed by dog-food labels. 'My rule used to be that if there were ingredients I couldn't pronounce, I wouldn't touch it. After a while, there was hardly a word I recognised.'

Having stayed in such good shape well into my middle age, I applaud the discipline he introduced into my life. Left to my own devices, I'd have happily existed on my sister Terry's favourite food: burgers, pizza, chicken nuggets, and, of course, sausages.

Not to mention Mom's outrageously good Cuban flan.

She, too, played an increasingly big role in my care; I especially valued her advice on grooming, because no one looks better than Mercy. That woman is in peak condition day and night. I don't know how she does it. If she'd had four legs, she'd have stolen Best in Show at Westminster or Crufts in any given year.

It was Mercy who took me to a pet dentist to have my teeth whitened. I don't remember much about that experience, except falling asleep as a pretty nurse stroked my ears. When I woke up, all I could taste in my mouth for days was peppermint.

'Once you get into movies, Uggie,' Mercy told me knowingly, 'you'll appreciate the importance of a good dental regime. Especially in your close-ups.'

She was right. I was not a fan of sunglasses – which never sat very comfortably on my furry snout – but there were many occasions when they saved me from a dazzling set of gnashers glinting down at me from above, and threatening to burn my retinas.

And yes, I mean you, Mr Clooney.

## ACTING IS ALL ABOUT HONESTY. IF YOU CAN FAKE THAT, YOU'VE GOT IT MADE.
### *George Burns*

When Dad drove me downtown for my first movie audition, I was excited to show off all the hard work he'd put into honing my natural talents. I also welcomed any extra time spent alone with him, now that he had a mate and pup of his own, plus more animals at home than ever, all vying for his attention.

Yes, it's true: although it irked me a little, I wasn't his only star. Nor was I his first movie dog. Andy had done great work ahead of me, and by the time I came along, Omar had an impressive CV of his own. He went on to work with two Rottweilers (and Mark Wahlberg) in *Four Brothers*, a Doberman (and Kevin Spacey) for a magazine spread, an American bulldog (and Kiefer Sutherland) in *24*, and a 'rabid' Malinois – a Belgian shepherd – (and Halle Berry) in *Their Eyes Were Watching God*.

In the Halle Berry movie, Omar was badly bruised by the Malinois, which wasn't his. The scene was extremely tense, and the dog was encouraged to be extremely aggressive in a situation with a lot of noise from wind and rain machines. Omar was offered a bonus if he'd let the dog bite him with very little padding on his arm and, boy, did he earn that money!

When I heard what happened, I wanted to chew the balls off that crazy Belgian.

Far less demanding was the small, independent picture for which Omar first put me up. Entitled *Mr Fix It*, the storyline told of a man who fixed relationships for others, but couldn't seem to fix his own. The role I was trying for was 'Max', a former stud-farm terrier that the male lead picked from a pound, just so he could attract a dog-loving girl he had his eye on. I was supposed to woo the girl's white poodle 'Maxine' and help him get his mate.

According to Omar, the director wanted 'smart'. No acting required!

'There's a scene where he'll have to be driven away in a cage on the back of a truck by someone from Dog Control,' said the man in charge of hiring. 'Can he look miserable in that?'

'Sure, and with genuine feeling. He nearly ended up in a pound himself,' Omar replied.

'How will he react when he sees a couple having sex?' the man asked, eyeing me suspiciously. 'He won't bite the male lead or anything, will he?'

Omar laughed. 'Well, he sleeps on our bed every night and he hasn't attacked me yet!'

I got the part, and Gordo was picked for a walk-on role, too.

To be honest, the job wasn't especially challenging. I had to dig up a bone and present it to the puffed-up poodle. I had to snuggle next to her and place a paw around her. Best of all, there was a comic humping scene with her – and a shapely golden retriever, too. That was a cinch.

The funniest part was having to lick Gordo's butt (smeared in baby food), as the human actor delivered the line, 'He's studying to be a proctologist.'

Mostly, though, I had to sit and look interested and cock my head as if listening, which is what I did most days anyway. It was no sweat.

The movie was shot at various locations around Los Angeles, and I loved every minute of it – especially all the attention the humans gave me, kissing and cuddling me or constantly telling Omar, 'Aw, he's so cute!' Best of all, though, was the catering truck. Hot food whenever I wanted? That was the life.

Omar followed me as I raced to the truck one day after a shoot and watched open-mouthed as I did my sit-up-and-beg, bow, head-under-my-paw routine, all on my own.

'What the – ?' he cried, as everyone started laughing and throwing me food. Then he wagged his finger at me. 'Very funny, Uggie, but you know you have to be a little hungry or one of your motivations is gone,' he added, as I caught another flying sausage in one athletic leap.

'Seriously, guys,' he told my new fan club, chuckling to himself as I did a couple of victory rolls, 'you've got to stop feeding him. I really do have to monitor his food intake.'

He was right, of course. I had to be fed just enough, but not so much that I'd get tired, fall asleep, or refuse to work. What Dad didn't know yet was that I had already reached the magic point in an actor's career, when he does what is expected of him for the intrinsic reward of the work itself, and not just for the pay.

Earning my sausages on the set of
*Mr Fix It* with David Boreanaz.

My co-stars included David Boreanaz, who played a character called Lance Valenteen (a name not a million miles away from *The Artist*'s George Valentin, spookily). I'd seen him in a few episodes of *Buffy the Vampire Slayer* on TV, so I felt like I already knew him. The female lead was the lovely Alana de la Garza, who smelled like bubblegum. She and I spent most of her scenes together kissing and cuddling. Even though I felt a little disloyal to Momma Mercy, I was by then a dedicated fan of Method acting. I set aside my misgivings and committed myself fully to my character.

Although I think it would be fair to say that *Mr Fix It* didn't allow me to explore anything approaching my full range, Omar was clearly impressed with how quickly I understood what was required of me and how well I behaved on set – unless, of course, I was anywhere near the catering truck.

'I was amazed,' he recounted recently. 'Uggie was such a natural. When he was on set and supposed to do something, he didn't hesitate. He understood very quickly what needed to be done for a shot, just like any professional who goes and does his thing. I had other dogs who were better at tricks, but I knew right from the beginning that Uggie was my best actor.'

**THE GREAT PLEASURE OF A DOG IS THAT
YOU MAY MAKE A FOOL OF YOURSELF
WITH HIM AND NOT ONLY WILL HE NOT
SCOLD YOU, BUT HE WILL MAKE A
FOOL OF HIMSELF TOO.**
*Samuel Butler*

Confident that he could get me more work, Dad sent my portfolio to some more agencies, and we trotted off together to numerous auditions. Every actor knows what a soul-destroying business auditioning can be. No matter how much confidence you may have in your own abilities, or how much you psych yourself up for the part, it is crushing to be rejected time and again for something over which you have no control:

Too short.

Too fat.

Too thin.

Too hairy.

The wrong sex.

The wrong 'type'.

I tried not to be bitter, but the rejection was hard for a budding young star such as myself. Some of the most cutting comments related to my limited ability to express human emotions.

'He doesn't look sad enough,' one director said.

'Can't you make him laugh?' asked another.

'Does he shed tears?'

'Can he do avarice?'

I began sniffing out the competition and wondered if I was crazy even to consider a career in Hollywood. There were sleek Weimaraners, immaculately groomed collies, glossy Dobermans, and fluffy Lhasa apsos. I marked my own territory thoroughly, but my amateurish claim was almost certainly lost in the professional mélange.

In the movie industry, trends come and go (usually based on previous successes) and the fashion in canine actors is no exception. Pugs had been far more popular since *Men in Black*, and *Hotel for Dogs*. The movie *Marley & Me* had brought Labrador retrievers back into play. Chihuahuas were hot, thanks to *Transformers* and *Legally Blonde* (with darling Reese!). Beagles had never really been out of favour since the cartoon pooch Snoopy stole the world's hearts.

I thought of all the other great historical hounds in the industry, like Buck from *Call of the Wild*, Strongheart in *White Fang*, or Beasley in *Turner & Hooch*, and then I'd catch a glimpse of myself in the mirror. An unremarkable, wire-haired Jack Russell that everyone said was too short to be a leading man looked back. I didn't exactly see an A-lister.

Am I an A-lister?

Unemployed, a terrier is never happy, and the frustration started to get to me. My street performances still drew the crowds, but I wanted more. Dejected and out of work, I'd return home from the canine cattle call with Omar (who never made me feel like anything other than Academy Award-winning material) and settle down in front of the TV, which is where I tend to do my best thinking.

Licking my wounds, I'd remind myself how fortunate I was even to be padding around on this planet after Cat-Gate. Stanislavski famously reported that there were 'no small parts, only small actors'.

Well, I was one small actor. But I would get a big part one day. I had to keep believing that.

## WHAT COUNTS IS NOT NECESSARILY THE SIZE OF THE DOG IN THE FIGHT, IT'S THE SIZE OF THE FIGHT IN THE DOG.
### *Dwight D. Eisenhower*

Luckily for me, the stars had plans. As word about how good I was hit the street, I became much more in demand for commercials, and then three more movie roles beckoned. They included a romantic, offbeat comedy called *What's Up Scarlet?* (offered to me on the spot on the streets of Santa Monica), a Disney movie called *Life is Ruff*, followed by a picture entitled *Wassup Rockers*.

*What's Up Scarlet?* was fun because I wasn't the only member of our pack to be picked. Gordo, Chata, and Brando also got in on the act, all of us playing the adored pets of a workaholic woman living with a controlling mother. The part wasn't especially demanding, and some of my best work ended up on the cutting-room floor. Gordo had far better exposure than me, for which I was grateful, for that gentle old bonehead deserved all the breaks he could get.

In *Life is Ruff*, my character was an award-winning pure-bred pet of an aristocratic teenager. That was more like it. I was named 'Jean-Jacques St Germain des Prés', of all things. As the reigning champion of several dog shows, I had to show off my skills catching Frisbees and jumping through hoops. I also had to attack a skateboarding kid and bite him on the ankle. I was smeared in wet mud as my human was dragged through a flower bed. In two separate scenes, I was pitched one-on-one against a scruffy stray named Tyco in a dog agility course (in which Omar and Gordo also had cameo roles).

I had so much fun in those sequences. Not only did I get to show how fleet of foot I was, as I weaved around obstacles and jumped over fences, flying through the air like a bird, but I also swam across a pool, rolled over repeatedly, and took a bow.

All that, and payment, too?

Heck, I loved show business!

In *Wassup Rockers*, which was about a group of South American kids in South Los Angeles, I had little more than a passing role, although I did get to bite a kid on the butt and chase him over a wall. Once again, I did all my own stunts. I also had to connect with what I thought of as my inner 'Urban Uggie', chiefly because – against my own personal moral code – I had to hump an actress's leg. It was not work of which I was especially proud.

Seeing how some of the other animal coaches worked on set, I soon realised that Omar was different and special. While many of them were highly protective of their charges and would cry things like 'Don't touch my dog!' or 'Don't look at my animal when he's working!' Omar was the exact opposite. He allowed everyone to pet and stroke me – he even encouraged it.

'Go ahead and pick him up if you want to,' he'd say. 'I like Uggie to be totally happy with everyone around him, no matter who it is. It's an important part of his socialisation.'

Carried along on a sea of caressing hands, I never once complained.

Even though I was a veteran of four movies, my demands on set were minimal. As Omar explained to one producer who asked for my 'rider' (the official list of an actor's requirements), 'The main thing is that Uggie doesn't get overworked or burnt out during shoots, because that can affect him physically, as well as his training. We need a space to let him rest. We also need plenty of bottled water, plus air conditioning if it's hot, and heat in the winter. I'll take care of everything else.'

I'm not proud of it now, but I have to admit that the film-star treatment did begin to affect me, and I sometimes allowed the stardom to go to my head. It happens all too often in Hollywood, when success comes too quickly for a young actor, but that's still no excuse. Even though I was living at home and had the steadying influence of a kind and loving family, I found myself swept along by all the flattery and attention and some-times got carried away.

Food had become synonymous in my mind with reward, and there was a small part of me that craved even more. On one trip to The Ivy in Beverly Hills with British celebrity photographer Rupert Thorpe and his wife Michelle, I became so overexcited at being fed Kobe beef that I almost got us kicked out of the restaurant.

What sparked my
eating disorder.

Like many stars who overeat, drink too much, or occasionally starve themselves once they make it to the big time, I became caught up. Confused by conflicting signals, seeking some form of control, I lost my way for a while.

That's my excuse for Binge-Gate, anyway.

One night, Mom and Dad had been out for the evening, and when they came home, they found me lying lethargic on the bed, my stomach pleasantly stretched.

'What's up, buddy?' Omar asked, stroking my hot little head. He told Mercy, 'Uggie doesn't look so good. I'm worried.'

Mercy (who was always the smartest), eyed me suspiciously. 'Do you think he could have eaten something he wasn't meant to?' she asked. I refused to dignify her accusation with any response, and I continued to peer sorrowfully into Omar's eyes.

'No! What could he have eaten? We haven't left anything lying around.'

His mate narrowed her eyes and then began a hunt around the house for any evidence. I swear she has some bloodhound in her Cuban ancestry. As I lay in a dead faint, accepting Omar's kisses, she rummaged under the bed and emerged with a triumphant 'Ha!'

In her hand she held an empty pack of ham and cheese, the plastic ripped open, its contents gone. Omar frowned, not sure if the evidence was conclusive enough.

'Uggie?' he questioned, unwilling to believe what was being waved in front of his eyes.

I closed my eyes and slid further down the duvet.

Turning to Mercy, Dad said, 'But where could he have got that from?'

'It was in the fridge!' she declared.

Together, they marched into the kitchen to search for more clues to prove or disprove my guilt. The refrigerator door was closed, the hand towel Mercy often draped on the handle still in place. The floor was clean. There was no trace of any crime.

Perplexed, the two of them opened the door and peered inside. There, on the lowest glass shelf – always kept so spotlessly clean by Mom – was all the forensic evidence she needed.

Frozen in silhouette were two terrier-sized paw prints.

It took them a while, but they finally figured out what I'd done. Having been drawn to the kitchen by impulses beyond my control, I sniffed for sustenance and considered the situation with the scrutiny of a Baskerville hound. When I had assessed my best chance of reward, I grabbed the towel looped around the fridge door handle between my terrier teeth and began to yank on it.

There had to be just enough pressure to pull the door open, but if I tugged too hard, then the towel could slip off the handle and ruin my plan. Applying the correct amount of leverage, I slid backwards just enough to release the handle and swing open the heavy door.

I knew exactly what I was doing, because that wasn't my first foray into the chilly larder. It was, however, the first time I was caught, and only because the pack of ham and cheese lay on a slightly higher shelf, which meant I had to step up and reach it. Once I had my prize in my jaws, I cat-footed it back to the bedroom and hid under the bed, so that fat Popeye and Gordo couldn't get to it or me. It only took a few seconds to rip the packet open and wolf down my snack.

Once Mom and Dad had figured it out, they didn't need a police line-up. My guilt was written as clear as a pawprint on the refrigerator shelf.

The Binge-Gate episode which
led me to rehab.

To my dismay, the towel was removed to another position, never to return. My binge-eating phase was abruptly stopped. Mom and Dad made me go cold turkey (without the cold turkey, which I also love).

After a few days of rehab, I finally recovered enough from my misdemeanour and vowed to make it up to them. I was earning some real money at last – although it was nothing like what people might think. Human actors not only get a substantial fee for the work they put into a movie, they are normally entitled to a share of the profits through residuals.

Animal actors get no such deals.

We are paid a daily fee for the work we put in (which depends on experience and reputation) and our trainers are similarly reimbursed. After that – no matter how successful the movie might become – we receive no further bonuses. If we are asked to help promote the picture in any subsequent press junket, then we can charge the same daily rate, but that is it. If we are lucky, we may get a few bonus treats, a poster or two, or maybe a free DVD thrown in. We might even be invited to some private screenings and events.

It can be a good living, if you keep busy and get plenty of offers. But if there are long periods of unemployment between engagements, then you need to learn to stash your kibble.

Luckily for me, I'd never really been out of work. With my growing income from movies and commercials, I decided to treat my human and animal family to a new giant-sized bed (big Gordo was especially grateful for the extra room).

We moved to a bigger house with a larger yard for skateboarding and a better pool for water sports. Once again, and in spite of Binge-Gate, I was forgiven by all. My pole position was unassailable, and I was still the first in line when it came to massages, pawdicures, and treats.

When Mom and Dad threw a party at the house on New Year's Eve, I naturally assumed that all the fuss and excitement was about me. Surely all the well-groomed guests eating plates of delicious-smelling food were there to help celebrate my newfound status as a leading cinematic canine?

Convinced that I was the reason for the celebration, I paraded around the house like a show dog, straining my neck to catch the eyes and compliments of the chattering humans. I even performed a few routines to make them notice me. Some did, and I earned myself a couple of sausage rolls and a slice of pizza. Mostly, though, they ignored me, which I thought was rather rude, considering I'd paid for it all.

Emotionally bruised, I sank down in a corner, away from the forest of legs that seemed to be jiggling around to a Shania Twain record (Omar and Mercy loved Shania). Licking my paws, I contemplated the fickleness of fame. So much for star status. I felt a wave of insecurity and fresh cravings sweep over me.

A woman wandered over, so I looked up hopefully. Instead of patting me or smothering me with kisses as I'd hoped, she set down on the floor a full glass of champagne and wandered off to join in dancing.

Curious, I sniffed and peered at the golden bubbles dancing inside the glass, as if in time to the thumping beat. Their motion was mesmerising. Getting up, I got a little closer and lowered my nose over them until they popped in my nostrils. Shaking my head in surprise, I extended the tip of my tongue and allowed them to tickle it. Moving closer, I placed my forepaws firmly on the base of the glass either side of the stem and began to lap at the sparkling human drink.

I can't say that I especially enjoyed my first sip. It was sweeter than anything I was accustomed to, and with a slightly bitter aftertaste. I'd seen how much the humans liked it, though, and wondered if it might be an acquired taste. After all, I hadn't known how great pizza was until I tried it.

In a matter of minutes, the fizzing glass was empty, and I sat back licking my lips and wondering why someone had turned the music up.

The room seemed to get much hotter, too. It must have been all those sweating bodies. I decided that I needed some fresh air and water, but when I went to stand up, something strange happened. My legs didn't work so well. In fact, my front left gave way under me and I crashed forwards onto the empty glass.

'Oops!' someone nearby said, lifting it out of the way. 'Are you okay, pal?'

Then the woman who'd left the bubbly there stepped forward and asked, 'Did he drink my champagne?' I looked up to see two of her; her faces strangely close together and floating alarmingly. 'Hey, Omar!' she called. 'Uggie's drunk!'

I didn't know what 'drunk' was, but I knew I wasn't feeling so good. Omar hurried over and scooped me up in his arms and carried me outside for some air. Unfortunately, that only made me feel worse, so I staggered back inside, almost falling again as I went.

'It's bedtime for you, buddy,' Omar told me, laughing.

Good idea.

The next thing I knew, I was sprawled across the duvet, my eyes squeezed shut to stop the room from spinning. He sat with me for a while and stroked my head, until I finally drifted off to sleep.

I was out cold for eight hours straight, and I woke up the next morning feeling less than well. The inside of my mouth tasted like the bottom of Mango's cage. Leaving Mom and Dad sleeping, I wandered downstairs to get a drink of water and found the house in a rare state of disarray. Empty glasses littered every surface, and there were morsels of party food on the carpet. Popeye and Gordo were doing a good job of cleaning them up. Oddly, I didn't feel inclined to help – even when I spotted a half-eaten sausage roll.

Collapsing onto my usual spot on the couch, I couldn't even be bothered to paw the remote control. I didn't need the noise. Instead, I stared at my own sorry reflection in the dark glass of the screen and pondered how close I had come to succumbing to my movie-star cravings.

It was a new year and time for a fresh start. I had to put those difficult days behind me. I closed my eyes and prayed that the coming year would bring me nothing but pure, refreshing water and blissful peace.

## SOME OF MY BEST LEADING MEN HAVE
## BEEN DOGS AND HORSES.
### *Elizabeth Taylor*

In 2009, a friend of Omar's heard that a French director was looking for a dog for a movie that was to be shot in Hollywood. 'When I saw that the script called for a really talented Jack Russell, I thought Uggie would be perfect for this movie,' she told him.

Her name was Sarah Clifford, and I'd been signed with her company, Animal Savvy, for a number of years. 'There were only a few dogs I knew of who could do this,' she said later. 'The dog was a star. He would have to perform really big, circus-y routines and be with the main character on a stage. Uggie was the best I knew for the role.' With that in mind, she sent the film company some videos of me and told Omar to expect a call, but the call never came.

Not one to sit on my haunches, I took off with Omar on tour as part of *The Incredible Dogs Show*, an event he'd been involved in for years. Designed to raise money and awareness for rescue dogs, the show – held in one of the largest big tops in the world – featured some of the most versatile hounds I knew; almost all of them saved from shelters or pounds.

Along with Julio, Popeye, and Jumpy from my pack, we teamed up on the tour with Bella the Frisbee Dog World Champion; Carrie the dancing retriever; Grit, an Australian cattle dog who regarded Frisbees much as I regarded parrots; Jasmine, a world-class Frisbee champion who was rescued from a freeway, and Harley, a flyball champ. In a two-hour show of heart-stopping action, we toured Puerto Rico, Venezuela, and the Dominican Republic, showing off our agility skills and amazing repertoire of routines.

I loved that gig, and enjoyed every minute of being on the road, especially the 'meet and greet' at the end, where everyone wanted to pat or stroke me, shake my paw, or have their photo taken with me. It was all part of the show's mission to promote the adoption of unwanted dogs.

Fans would flock around and, before too long, ask Omar for his advice. 'My dog's really smart,' I'd hear people tell him again and again. 'I think he could do all those tricks with a bit of training.' Or they might say, 'My Labrador could skateboard, I'm sure. How can I get her into show business?'

Dad was always polite and constantly encouraged enthusiasm for any animal, but he couldn't allow people to think that the work we did was easy. He knew they'd get frustrated with the lack of progress and might take it out on the dog. He'd usually advise, 'It takes years to train an animal like this, working long hours every single day. Even if you're prepared to put in the time, you can still find yourself with a dog that simply can't perform under pressure. There's much more to this than people think.'

Yeah. We're the professionals – so go fetch a stick!

Being on tour, what I wasn't so keen on was having to travel 'cargo' on flights between different countries. This involved being locked into a crate and placed on a conveyor belt like so much baggage, then loaded into the hold, while Omar sat in a comfy seat up top. So much for show business! After a few trips, though, I grew accustomed to the drill: the darkness, cramped conditions, phenomenal noise, and the stench of aviation fuel. I wisely used the time to catch up on my beauty sleep or attend to some personal grooming. It was reassuring to have some of the guys there with me, too.

With my canine capacity for infinite forgiveness, I greeted Omar exuberantly whenever he rescued me from the cargo area in arrivals. I'd bark and bark until released from my crate, and then I'd jump up and lick him all over, just to let him know that he could claim my air miles.

**18**

BE NOT TOO TAME NEITHER BUT LET
YOUR OWN DISCRETION BE YOUR
TUTOR. SUIT THE ACTION TO THE WORD;
THE WORD TO THE ACTION.
*William Shakespeare*

Back in LA, I was offered the opportunity to try out for a part in a big-budget movie entitled *Water for Elephants*. It was to be based on a bestselling novel about an American travelling circus during the Great Depression.

When Omar and I arrived for the audition at a production office downtown, though, we found scores of hopeful Jack Russells waiting in line with their humans.

'Keep calm, buddy,' he told me when he saw how much competition I'd be up against. There were smooth-coats and rough-coats, long-legged Parsons, all-white specimens, several with patches, and a few hybrid black and tans. There were some that looked more like foxhounds, and many mixed breeds that clearly came from questionable pedigree.

Most were well groomed, others brazenly scruffy. I fell somewhere inbetween.

I don't believe that Omar kept anything from me deliberately, but it wasn't until I showed the director my extensive range of acting skills that it was revealed to me that the part was for a she-dog named Queenie. My little wet nose was quite put out of joint, I can tell you. After years of scorning Pal for playing Lassie, had I really sunk to his level?

Still, work was work.

In spite of what must surely have been my sullen expression (or perhaps because of it), the director Francis Lawrence loved me and immediately offered me the role. Omar was clearly thrilled, so I quickly realised I'd have to man up and play a female.

Filming took place in the summer of 2009, mostly out in the desert country of Fillmore in Ventura County, California. There were also a few shots done on the Fox lot, and at locations in Tennessee. The leading roles of Marlena and Jacob had already been cast, with Reese Witherspoon playing the glamorous performing wife of the circus owner, and Robert Pattinson playing the drifter who provides the love interest.

Some of the harsher film critics said afterwards that although they enjoyed the movie, they felt there was a 'lack of romantic chemistry' between the two actors. The truth behind that, I can now reveal, is that Miss Witherspoon only had eyes for me (oh, all right, and occasionally for my pack brother Popeye).

My character, Queenie, may have spent most of 'her' time in the company of a diminutive circus-hand named Kinko, but

Reese and I did appear in quite a few scenes together – not all of which made the final cut. Recently divorced and with two small children, surely Miss W. was in need of a new leading male in her life?

Gender-bending on the set
of *Water for Elephants*.

Even though she was a big movie actress, with starring roles in *Legally Blonde*, *Vanity Fair*, *Sweet Home Alabama*, and *Walk the Line*, dear Reese did her best to put me at ease. She told me how much she loved animals and that she had many pets at home. She was extremely generous as a fellow actor, always making sure I was free to give a scene my best performance.

I adored her.

On or off screen, the atmosphere between us was electrically charged.

RPattz didn't stand a chance.

I'd watched several television programmes in my time about some of the great Hollywood romances that have developed between screen idols. It has always been far more common than people realise, especially when two actors are working so closely together for such an intense period of time.

Think of Garbo and Gilbert, Taylor and Burton, Pitt and Jolie, Hepburn and Tracey, Bogart and Bacall, Lady and the Tramp.

It happens.

What I didn't expect was for it to happen to me. At the ripe old age of 56 in human years, I had fallen in love for the first time, and with a human more than 20 years my junior. And, boy, did I fall.

*Water for Elephants* was a $38-million production for Twentieth Century Fox, and was much bigger than anything Omar and I had ever been involved in before. I was to be in quite a few scenes (not all of which made the final cut, sadly) and had to be on set most days for a full month.

The sheer size of the cast was staggering. There were more than 500 human actors and crew, and umpteen animals. There were acrobats, dwarves, and clowns. I also got to work alongside a 42-year-old elephant named Tai, who'd been in a few movies before and once appeared in a Britney Spears video (we've all got our skeletons in the closet).

By every rule in the animal kingdom, I should have been terrified of Tai, who towered above me like a skyscraper. She weighed more than 9,000 pounds and could have crushed me like a peanut beneath one of her enormous feet. But, even though Omar was careful to only allow me to admire her from a distance, I sensed from the moment I met her that Tai had the heart of a lamb.

Soft and gentle, she had eyelashes Mercy would have killed for and breath that smelled of freshly mown hay. The other end of her, however, wasn't quite so fragrant. Dear Tai was notoriously flatulent and once farted with such force – as Reese moved around behind her – that she nearly knocked my new love Reese off her feet.

The elephant also had a sweet tooth and would do almost anything for a jelly bean. I was envious of her dexterity with her trunk, which worked both as a hand and a nose. With it, she was forever exploring pockets, faces, and hands for treats. If a human ever hugged her trunk, she'd playfully hoist them 7 feet up into the air, just for fun.

It was later claimed that Tai had once been abused by humans. Taken five years earlier, secret film footage was released that showed her being given electric shocks with prodders and beaten with hooks, similar to the storyline of the movie, and a true case of life imitating art. The revelation upset everyone who knew and loved her.

I'm here to report that the movie's biggest star was treated with nothing but kindness on our set, and I was so impressed by her trainer Gary, who seemed just to whisper gently to her. With minimal encouragement, she'd play her part right on the money. She was loved and respected by all her fellow actors, especially Robert Pattinson, who reportedly only agreed to take the role after he'd met his pachyderm co-star.

Not that he wasn't good to me, too; he was forever stroking and kissing me.

Robert Pattinson and me in full character
mode in *Water for Elephants*.

(I know, I know. Steady, RPattzers).

From what I could tell, when he was around that gentle giant, however, his feelings for her were off the scale. Theirs was undoubtedly a deep and meaningful personal relationship. Even when she let one go, his love for her remained undiminished. Rumour had it that, when the movie ended, he wept and offered to adopt her, and even that he asked her out on a date.

Catching air in my early
days as a skateboarder.

**LEFT**
My lowly start as a street entertainer with Omar in Santa Monica.

**BELOW**
Allowing my pack to share our new king-size.

Ready for water-skiing with
Brando and Extreme Pete.

Waiting for directions
in the quicksand scene.

**LEFT**
Relaxing between scenes with co-star James Cromwell.

**BELOW**
In character and costume as 'Jack' with 'George Valentin' in *The Artist*.

**ABOVE**
Sharing the glory
at the Oscars with
Jean Dujardin.

**LEFT**
Golden Globe
Awards poster
trumpeting
our success.

**LEFT**
Playing it cool
with the love of
my life, Reese
Witherspoon.

**BELOW**
With Katy Perry,
who kissed a dog
and she liked it!

**LEFT**
Me and the gang relaxing by the pool after my retirement.

**BELOW**
Setting my pawprints in concrete outside Grauman's Chinese Theatre in Hollywood.

**19**

## MAN IS DOG'S IDEA OF
## WHAT GOD SHOULD BE.
### *Holbrook Jackson*

The menagerie of other animals on the set of the movie reminded me of a musical I'd once watched on TV with Gordo. It was called *Doctor Doolittle*, and the premise was that an eccentric doctor, played by Rex Harrison, had learned more than 500 animal languages.

As if.

Nobody could learn Squirrel – not even a human.

I felt a bit like Doctor Doolittle, though, as I walked around the set with Omar and mingled with llamas and horses, a buffalo, an extremely polite giraffe named Stanley, and a tiger named Serena (now that's what I called a cat). There was a hyena, two lionesses, a rather grumpy lion named Major, a bear, four leopards, two lion cubs, two wolves, four bad-breathed camels, and two kangaroos.

Omar was a little anxious at first. He'd seen me at my worst with Mango. He'd been told about Goat-Gate and he knew that, when it came to squirrels and pigeons, I could lose control. Not surprisingly, perhaps, he kept me on a leash to begin with. He wanted to watch how I responded to each of my fellow actors and make sure that I didn't feel threatened.

Taking a break on the set of
*Water for Elephants.*

He needn't have worried.
My bad-boy days were (almost) over.

What became my nemesis, though – and the only thing that marred the unadulterated bliss of being near Miss W. – were four braying zebras named Widowmaker, Ace, Stripes, and Zac. Just as with all the other creatures, Omar took me to meet them in their enclosure before filming. I sniffed at the weird-looking horses, and they sniffed back at me. I didn't much like their toothy faces or their strange mohawk manes, and I guess it must have showed, because one of them made a sudden lunge for me.

Light on my paws, I jerked away, but only just in time. Its jaws snapped shut like an alligator's, and I was assaulted with compost breath. Deciding to take the higher moral ground, I pretended to ignore it. I'd heard that a few of the crew were scared of the zebras, and I didn't want them to think an old hand like me was, too. Instead, I showed my general disdain by leaving an abusive p-mail for them, before turning and walking away.

Point made.

Three days later, we were shooting in the big top, which had been erected in the middle of nowhere, near a town called Piru, in East Ventura County. It was the part of the movie where the circus parade marches into the tent full of eagerly awaiting people, just before the show begins. The clowns, performers, and acrobats all walked in together, smiling and waving, leading their animals.

My co-star – a delightful actor named Mark Povinelli, who was playing 'Kinko' – was dressed up like a prison warder to lead me in. Omar got to wear the same kind of outfit, in case he needed to be seen on camera, too. I was wearing a similar uniform and a little striped pillbox hat, which I felt was a little busy for my subtle markings.

Omar and me in costume on the set
of *Water for Elephants*.

I guess I was off stripes altogether, because our position in the parade was right behind those zany zebras, and we were expected to pad in their hoof prints. Fearing the worst as we set off, I dragged my paws. Sure enough, those mealy-mouthed African equids pooped right in our path, just as we set off. To avoid a steaming pile of droppings, I had to do a quick side-step. I was seeing red, and I'm afraid to admit that I had one of my mad-dog moments: I went for their ankles, completely forgetting I was on a leash. In my frenzy, I almost dislocated poor Mark's shoulder, and very nearly choked off the breath in my own throat.

With each new take we had to do (and not only because of me, I hasten to add), the convict-striped grass-grazers behaved just as badly, and they got to me every time. I was helpless in the face of my fury, driven by the Law of Tooth and Claw. There was so much unresolved conflict between us that no amount of cajoling or soothing could calm me down.

Zebra-Gate was not my finest hour. Mark and I ended up being moved to a prime spot behind Stanley the giraffe, which was a far better position anyway. His legs were so long that I had a much-improved view of the proceedings, and Stanley was far too well mannered to dump on me from any height.

As I am in a confessional frame of mind, now is probably the time to reveal, for the first time, and exclusively, my greatest weakness as a professional performer. That is what memoirs are for, after all. It is a chance for a celebrity to tell the truth at last and set the record straight.

Okay then, dogs and she-dogs, here's the dirt.

Whenever I am instructed to sleep, I do precisely that, which Omar, the director, and I all felt made for a deeply convincing shot. Due to some sort of genetic soft-palate problem common with a lot of terriers, however, I snore.

And I mean like an elephant in heat.

This led to numerous takes of one scene in *Water for Elephants*, when Robert got the giggles because he couldn't hear himself speak his lines above my stentorian snuffles. Omar had to shake me awake and start again.

With my co-star Mark Povinelli
in *Water for Elephants*.

Thankfully, dear Reese wasn't in those scenes, so I didn't embarrass myself in front of her.

Snoring retakes aside, making that movie was one of the greatest experiences of my life. Everyone working on it bonded so well (apart from the hateful zebras). I especially loved the light and the locations, the crew and, of course, the catering team.

Mark Povinelli was such a dream of an actor to work with, and he and I really connected – not only as fellow thespians, but also because we were both smaller than average and on the fringes of mainstream society. He said some lovely things about me to the press afterwards, including the claim that I was 'probably the most talented character [he] worked with on set'.

I must have impressed him, because he so believed that I was 'Queenie' that he often got confused about my gender, calling me 'good girl' and 'good boy' alternately. He added, '[Queenie] never missed a cue; she never missed a performing trick. If there was ever a time that the scene didn't work, it was because I messed up the command, not that Queenie didn't deliver. Queenie is a total pro.'

Reese, too, reportedly wept when filming was over, because – just like the rest of us – she so didn't want it to end. She hated having to say goodbye to Tai, the cast, and crew – but especially (I like to think) me.

I, too, felt heartbroken by our forced separation. When I returned to LA and reality, all I could do was rest my head in my paws and whimper for days. Even though I was reunited with dear Gordo and the rest of the gang for a frenzy of mutual sniffing and grooming, I still ached inside. Mercy and Terry spoiled me rotten, but it took me months to get over the fact that I wouldn't be seeing Miss W. any time soon.

If only she would call.

To rub salt into my wounds, two strange dogs – a chocolate Labrador named Hank and a German shepherd called Nashville – suddenly appeared in our midst. Omar occasionally took in other people's pets for a week or so, to give them some basic obedience training. Then he'd take them back to the owner and coach them in how to handle them.

The newcomers were nice enough (if a little frisky at first). Once I'd established my status as top dog, they quickly settled in. I was a tad jealous when Omar spent so much time with them in the back yard or at the park, but I got it. This was all part of what Dad did for a living, and if it paid for my sausages, then who was I to complain?

They responded well to his instructions and he seemed pleased. We got used to having them around and enjoyed their company. As with all these visiting dogs, though, it was over too soon, and we braced ourselves to say goodbye. Sure enough, one afternoon, I heard Dad calling up their owner to tell her that he'd be returning them soon.

'Miss Witherspoon?' he said, as I leapt out of my bed like a jack-in-the-box. 'Hank and Nashville are ready to come home now.'

'They're Reese's dogs?' I barked incredulously, as I cocked my head to listen more closely.

'Yes, they've been great,' he told her. 'They've learned a lot.' Then he laughed. 'No, they aren't quite as well trained as Uggie, but I think you'll be pleased.'

She wanted them to be as well trained as me? Wow!

I ran around the house to find her animals, my head forward and down. When I finally located them by the pool, I forensically examined each of them with my nose. They'd been with us for well over a week, but when I thrust my snout deep into the soft fur behind Nashville's ear, I was convinced I could actually detect the fragrant hand of Reese on him.

*Mon Dieu!*

I snorted joyfully at the smell.

Appalled that I hadn't appreciated their connection to my greatest love sooner, I bowed down before those two canine gods of Hollywoodland and offered them my humblest regards. Fetching my favourite squeaky skunk, I dropped it at Nashville's paws like an offering. He just tilted his head, stared at me, and then ran three times round me in a happy circle, barking and wagging his tail.

Leaning against Hank's sleek flank, I washed his ears with the care of a beauty therapist, in the hope that Reese might pick up something of my unique scent on him and remember that I existed. As Omar gathered together their belongings, I licked them both all over (the closest I could get to kissing her), and then it was time for them to go.

All I could do was watch with a wistful sigh as they were driven away, into the arms of the woman I loved.

## MY LITTLE DOG –
## A HEARTBEAT AT MY FEET.
### *Edith Wharton*

Health issues are a risk for any high-profile performer at the peak of his profession. When you're riding the crest of the wave (and I knew what that felt like for real), the physical and mental strain can be intense. Although I loved every minute of my craft, the truth was I wasn't getting any younger.

Downtime became increasingly important to me, and Omar was zealous in making sure that I rested well before, during, and after each new job. He was careful not to spoil me too much (that was Mercy and Terry's department), but he did take tender care of his big new star.

As always, I slumbered on the bed or sprawled on the couch watching TV for much of the day. My diet was still regulated, but hot dogs were allowed on special occasions (even if some were vegetarian). Daily workouts, whenever I felt up to it, included skateboarding, swimming in the pool, or ball games at the park.

Unbeknownst to me, though, Omar had noticed something I hadn't. During the filming of *Water for Elephants*, he'd spotted a slight tremor in my back legs, and then my front ones, too, whenever I sat up on my haunches or had any walk-on parts. To begin with, he worried that I might have been feeling the cold. He knew it wasn't because I was nervous. Personally, if I'd noticed it at all, I put it down to the trembling of my heart for my one true love.

'I think we need to get you checked out, *muchacho*,' he told me one day with a kiss. Then he took me to my least favourite place – the veterinary clinic – for a battery of tests to try to find out what the problem was.

Wrinkling my nose at the smells of disinfectant, urine, and worse, to my great indignation I was poked and prodded, jabbed repeatedly with needles, forced to pee into a dish, X-rayed, and strapped down in something called an MRI scanner.

So much for star treatment.

'Could be arthritis, Omar,' the vet told him at first. 'It's common in an eight-year-old, especially one who's had such an active life.'

While he was waiting for the results of all the tests, Omar put me on a regimen of acupuncture, chiropractic treatments, homeopathy, and massage, which was to become a regular feature of my life from then on. I didn't mind one bit of it, especially when the therapists were women whose soft hands smelled of eucalyptus.

There was life in the old boy yet.

Or so I thought.

'One of his tests came back, and it showed that Uggie has a slightly enlarged prostate,' the vet told Omar on our next visit. 'I know you believe that full males make better working dogs because of the extra hormone boost, but I would strongly recommend that you have him neutered, in light of this.'

'Neutered?' Omar repeated. 'Seriously?'

I couldn't have put it better myself.

'I'm afraid so. An enlarged prostate is far more prone to infection which – although unlikely to turn malignant – can prove very uncomfortable for the animal.'

More uncomfortable than slicing off my doghood? I'd watched enough episodes of *Emergency Vets* to know just how uncomfortable that would be.

'Oh, I don't know,' Omar said, frowning.

That a boy! I panted heavily, looking from one to the other as if at a tennis match.

'I can't decide now. I'll need to take him home and discuss it with my wife.'

To express my viewpoint, I curled my lip at the vet as we left. That would be the end of that, I was convinced. Mercy wouldn't let them do anything like that to me.

Two days later, when I bobbed back to the surface from under a general anaesthetic like a shipwrecked sailor, I realised I'd been wrong. Mercy had shown no mercy, in spite of all her kisses of reassurance.

I'd been butchered and was no longer 'entire'.
It was the unkindest cut.

Feeling sorry for myself after
losing my doghood.

The place where my family jewels had once been was a stitched seam of soreness. I licked at it lamely and sighed, before tucking my tail firmly between my legs. My dog days were over before they'd really begun, and I'd been cut off in my prime – literally.

And that wasn't the worst of it. I'd already been rejected by Chata in favour of Andy. Even Greta, a poodle with satisfying symmetry that Dad had taken in for training, had only ever allowed me a bit of petting. The truth was that all the humping I'd ever done in my life had been on set and on demand.

Reese Witherspoon and I were above anything physical – ours was much more of a metaphysical relationship – but at least when I'd been with her, I'd been a full, virile male in every sense of the word.

Now I was impotent.

Useless.

A barren barker, whose noble bloodline would never be continued. I'd never get to see any little Uggie's frolicking in the park.

I buried my head in my paws and contemplated the terrible truth – I had never even lost my virginity!

Now I never would.

Omar looked as uneasy about the whole thing as I felt, and he did all he could to placate me. 'It's okay, buddy,' he said, holding my paw and being careful to stroke only the parts of me that didn't hurt. 'You'll soon be up to all your old tricks.'

I stared up at him doubtfully and crashed my head back down on the bed with a sigh. Terry curled up next to me and held me in her arms in sympathy.

'The good news is that if you make it to the big time, no crazy fan is going to crawl out of the bushes one day to claim she's the mother of your love-pup.'

I wagged my tail weakly and figured he was right.

He was also right about my recovery, which was speedy, thanks to the tender care he and the rest of my family lavished upon me.

Recovering from my surgery
with my 'sister' Terry.

Within a few days, I was up and about, and after a week I was back on my skateboard where, I was pleased to discover, the absence of an undercarriage made me even more aerodynamic.

## HAPPINESS TO A DOG IS WHAT LIES ON THE OTHER SIDE OF A DOOR.
### *Charlton Ogburn*

There was, however, an unforeseen development that took us all by surprise. On a follow-up trip to the vet, the bad news was delivered to Omar and Mercy.

'I'm afraid it looks like Uggie may have developed something called Shaking Dog Syndrome,' the physician said.

Omar looked concerned. 'What's that?'

'It's a generalised neurological disorder that occurs primarily in small white dogs, which is why it's sometimes referred to as Little White Shakers Syndrome. At the moment, Uggie has it very mildly, and I don't suppose he even notices it. But it is something that can get worse with time and may lead to limb weakness or even seizures.'

Mercy pressed her face close to mine and covered me in a cascade of her sweet-smelling hair. (The shedding I'd feared never proved to be much of a problem.)

'What can be done?'

'Quite a lot. It can be treated with meds, such as corticosteroids, which might clear it up right away. If not, then we can monitor him over the next few years and tailor his drugs accordingly.'

Omar began a steady stroking rhythm up and down my back – knowing how much that soothed me.

'But I don't understand,' he said. 'Why would he suddenly develop something like this?'

The vet shrugged. 'No one really knows. It could be related to his auto-immune system or something that develops with age. The good news is, it doesn't cause him any pain, and it won't affect his personality one iota.'

Omar looked at the vet and then at Mercy, who looked at Omar and then back at me. You could have cut the silence with a scalpel.

Picking up on the tension in the room, I stood up on my back legs and fell backwards in a fake death scene, lying completely still. It worked. Everyone burst into laughter.

'It would take more than a tremor or two to alter this dog's personality!' Omar declared proudly.

I was carried home like a prince and treated like a king for several days. Omar was clearly worried about me, because he cut back on my exercise and coaching. I missed the work at first, but I didn't mind so much if it meant I could spend several straight days glued to my favourite channels.

There were some great programmes on and some truly gifted actors. I'm no talent scout, but I especially admired the work of

Brigitte as Sally the French bulldog in *Modern Family* (who quite rightly went on to win a Golden Collar Award for Best Dog in a Television Series). I loved watching reruns of *Frasier* featuring 'Eddie', of course, and was always humbled by the rescue animals on *DogTown* on National Geographic. *Scooby-Doo* always cheered me up, and Rowlf the dog made *The Muppet Show* watchable for me.

The series *Terriers*, however, was a big disappointment, and *Parks and Recreation* wasn't what I'd hoped for at all.

Once Dad realised that my leg trembling wasn't constant and didn't bother me in the slightest, he began to relax. The massage and acupuncture continued, along with visits to the chiropractor, and everyone assured him I was doing great.

'I guess we can go back to work then, buddy,' he told me one day. 'I know how much you love it.'

Jumping up, I vocalised my delight and performed a couple of victory rolls. Being laid off for a while was okay but, like all great actors, I couldn't wait to get back into the spotlight.

Little did I know just how bright that spotlight would become.

## TO HIS DOG, EVERY MAN IS NAPOLEON; HENCE THE CONSTANT POPULARITY OF DOGS.
### *Aldous Huxley*

I had only ever heard good things about the French, even though I'd never met a human or animal from that distant European country. To start with, it was said that they loved their dogs so much that they frequently carried them around in their handbags and took them into fashionable restaurants to feed them *foie gras* (fancy chopped liver).

Rumour had it that they liked to keep their *chiens* immaculately groomed and showed immense sense in favouring smaller examples such as *moi*. Lines and proportions were important to the stylish French, and their dogs were often chosen for their ability to prance along at their sides like miniature dressage horses. I could do that!

Generally speaking, the French also allowed dogs on trains and planes, as well as full freedom in most public places. They didn't obsessively poop-scoop like the Brits and Americans and preferred instead to leave things to disappear in a *naturel* kind of way. They even had special motorised vacuum cleaners to collect it up called *caninettes*. Who knew?

Nor did the French fret about leashes too much. Those great advocates of *joie de vivre* believed that each dog should be a free spirit, allowed to roam, mingle, and mate with whichever new she-dog he happened to favour.

*Vive la révolution!*

What I didn't fully appreciate about the French was that, while all of the above was true in some cases, it was not nation-wide. It may seem difficult to believe, but there are some French humans who not only do not share their lives and homes with a pooch, but they don't even like dogs. *Sacrebleu!*

I made this startling discovery the day that a Frenchman came to our house in 2010. His name was Michel Hazanavicius, which – when pronounced – sounded to me just like a human sneeze. 'Monsieur H.', as I came to call him, was the director Omar had been tipped off about the previous year; the one who was look-ing for a Jack Russell for a role in his movie called *The Artist*.

Now, I have excellent manners, and, along with my room-mates, have been trained to be on my best behaviour whenever anyone comes to call. That means no barking, no humping, no jumping up, and definitely no chasing cats or parrots. Mom prided herself on our house not only being a fur-free zone, but so sweet-scented that no one would think they kept animals in the house.

(She did a terrific job, but then she didn't have our sense of smell.)

This visit was no exception, and I could tell Omar was a little nervous. He asked fellow coach Sarah Clifford to come over and help out, just in case. We usually went to see the directors for auditions, after all. They didn't usually come to see us. Maybe it was a French thing.

Posing on set with animal
wrangler Sarah Clifford.

Monsieur H. seemed nice enough, but I noticed that he didn't stroke me like most humans, and he kept his hands well above the licking line. Something was up. Then, not long after he arrived, he confessed to Omar, 'I am afraid that I am not a dog lover.'

I was shocked. So were the rest of the guys. For a moment, I thought Popeye might even take a piece out of him. We'd never met anyone who didn't like our kind before. Mom, Dad, and all their friends were positively doting. Almost all the humans I'd worked with had been most attentive. Even my previous humans had fed me and cleaned up after me, kept me warm and safe. They'd caressed me when I was good (or too sleepy to be bad). Even though they'd ultimately decided I was a pound-bound hound, they'd loved me, or they'd never have taken me in the first place.

Dad took me into a room with Sarah and our guest, so that we could talk privately. Or gesticulate, more correctly, which he did so enthusiastically that he was in danger of taking someone's eye out. Our visitor's accent was strange, and he sometimes had to struggle for the right word in English, as he flapped his arms around like Mango in a fit of parrot pique.

I could tell even Omar needed to concentrate, but we gradually learned that the plot of the Frenchman's picture revolved around a swashbuckling silent movie star (and his dog), whose career was threatened by the arrival of talking pictures. He asked Omar if I could show him my best routines, so that he could record them on his camcorder.

'Ready, buddy?' Omar primed me. 'Let's show everyone what we can do!'

It was strange to have to 'improv' in my own environment. I was worried that the impromptu nature of the request might hamper my work. I'd been on light duties for a while, due to my condition, and I was a little out of practice. But as soon as the camera started to roll, the star in me began to glimmer. I did everything right on the money – 'Sit', 'Stay', 'Down', 'Walk', 'Speak', 'Bang/Play Dead'. Omar was thrilled and more than a little relieved.

'Can you make him do that last trick again, please?' asked the director. 'The one where you pretend to shoot him and he falls backwards?'

Centring myself and drawing on my full gamut of emotions, I did as I was asked, really throwing myself into the part with every 'Bang!' and making it look as dramatic as I could. Then he asked me to do it again, and again. With each pratfall, I felt that I added even more pathos.

'*Très bon*,' our visitor said, smiling finally. 'I like that. I think I will be able to incorporate it into my screenplay.' He then revealed that not only was he directing the movie, but that he'd also written the script himself. Furthermore, his wife, Bérénice Bejo, would be the female lead, making it a family show.

Omar's first thought was much the same as mine: this would be a low-budget movie, if the director had to double up as the writer and cast his own wife. Not that I cared. All I could think of was: me, Uggie, making a direct contribution to the script?

Not since the days of Rin Tin Tin had a scriptwriter studied a dog's behaviour and tailored the screenplay to suit it.

Maybe I'd get a credit on the titles, or – better still – a bonus in sausages?

Sorry, *saucisses*.

Almost as an aside and as he was leaving, my new favourite person in the world informed us that his movie would be both silent and in black and white.

**A true artist needs no introduction.**

'Wow!' Omar exclaimed. 'That'll be cool.'

Personally, I didn't see what was so cool about it. Apart from the odd bark, most of my acting never stretched my vocal range anyway. As a mainly white dog with just a few patches of brown, I was accustomed to a monochrome existence.

The director also told us that his movie was to be filmed at several historic locations in and around Los Angeles, as a homage to the silent-movie era. 'If Uggie is chosen, he'll feature in almost every frame,' added Monsieur H. We were excited, but neither of us expected that much from the picture to begin with, to be honest.

'It's the kind of thing that'll probably only be shown in Europe or go straight to DVD,' I heard Omar telling Mercy afterwards. 'We'll have to ask for a tape or we may never get to see it.'

Little did he know.

**23**

WE TREAT OUR DOGS AS IF THEY
WERE ALMOST HUMAN; THAT IS
WHY THEY REALLY BECOME ALMOST
HUMAN IN THE END.
*C. S. Lewis*

With no word from France for a week or more, Omar heard about the chance of another movie role and sent in my photos and reel. He wasn't overly hopeful I'd get it, though. 'They're really looking for a long-coat,' he told me wearily.

When the production team came back and asked if they could see me anyway, he was surprised. 'He's probably not right, but we'd still like to take a meeting,' they said. Omar was given the address of a house in the Hollywood Hills, and off we trotted to show them what I could do.

'It's a pretty basic role,' a member of the staff informed us, looking me up and down. 'No tricks. He just has to look intelligent and get along with the actors.'

'Uggie is really smart and he gets along with everyone,' Omar told them confidently. (Well, apart from cats, goats, squirrels, parrots, and zebras, that is.) After a few minutes of studying me and watching me walk up and down a room, sit pretty, and act at sleeping (Omar shook me awake before I snored), they sighed and said, 'Sorry, but it's a no. Thanks for bringing him, but the dog we're looking for is something more rough-coated.'

'You win some, you lose some,' Omar said as he drove me home.

The character I was rejected for was named 'Cosmo', and the movie was entitled *Beginners*. I was disappointed at first, because there aren't that many good character parts around for Jack Russells. Most are corny or clichéd, and I was keen to find myself another role with real drama to it after my success in *Water for Elephants*.

In truth, though, we'd never really expected to get it, and – as Omar said – it wasn't meant to be.

Thankfully, a few days later, we got the call back from France. The news was good. I had been cast in the role of 'Jack', the canine sidekick to the male lead George Valentin, in the movie *The Artist*.

If I'd been picked for *Beginners*, we'd have had to turn the French one down.

Everything was written in the stars …

**24**

THE DOG HAS SELDOM BEEN
SUCCESSFUL IN PULLING MAN UP
TO ITS LEVEL OF SAGACITY, BUT MAN
HAS FREQUENTLY DRAGGED THE
DOG DOWN TO HIS.
*James Thurber*

Several months passed as the preparations for filming got underway. News filtered through to us, and we learned that no one had taken Monsieur H. seriously to begin with. The producer who eventually believed in him had put up his own money to fund what was considered to be a risky and unusual project.

Once they had everything in place, though, it was full steam ahead, and we waited to hear where we'd have to be, and when. Our film was one of the few to be shot in Hollywood that year, and we were finally given a date in the autumn of 2010. The production company sent us a copy of the script, which looked strange, because it had no dialogue. Having it, though, meant that we could go through it, scene by scene, and break down which of my acting talents could be best utilised for each take.

Omar had been warned that the six to eight weeks on set would be long, intense, and demanding. 'The dog needs to be 100 per cent ready to go,' he was told.

'You needn't worry,' he replied confidently. 'Uggie doesn't need any special training. He's already so good at what he does. I'll just have to do a little work with his understudies, in case they should be required.'

My pack brother Dash was my main understudy (and chief professional rival). Omar had found him advertised by a show-dog breeder in Arizona on the Internet. He'd been looking for a double for me in *Water for Elephants* when he spotted the puppies for sale. 'This one's young, but he looks a lot like Uggie,' Omar said, after studying the photos. But when he called the breeder, Dash had been sold. Luckily for Dash, his new owner decided to give him up soon afterwards, so Omar took him in.

'That's when I realised why she'd given Dash up so readily. He was terrified of everything and everyone, from bikes to people. The sight of another dog could send him to a different planet. He didn't even know how to play with a ball. The breeder had been so worried about her puppies contracting parvovirus that she hadn't let them socialise at all. I had a lot of work to do with this dog.'

Dash's crash course in socialisation began on the set of *Water for Elephants*. Omar brought him along a few times, so that the pampered house dog, who'd rarely put a nose out of doors, had to cope with every kind of creature and situation. He quickly manned up. By the time he was ready to start work on *The Artist*, he was still learning how to cope with people and noise, but apart from the odd snap at the boom microphones, the Jack did good.

Dude, another Jack Russell, was new on the scene and enlisted by Sarah Clifford as a spare understudy. He was especially lucky; he'd been rescued from a California animal shelter the day he was due to be euthanised. Nobody wanted him, because his legs were short, and he'd been rejected by potential owners time and again. Facially, though, he looked a lot like me. Thanks to that sole attribute, his luck changed. Not only did Sarah save him, but she gave him the chance to be a movie star.

So take heart, all you shelter inmates out there!

Omar's greater concern was that there was a part of the filming schedule when he couldn't be with me on set, because he'd already committed to going to South America for *The Incredible Dogs Show* (albeit with a diminished cast). As Sarah had also been hired for *The Artist* to help Omar with me and the other dogs, she'd be in charge when he went away. Dad would just have to make sure she and I were completely comfortable with each other.

All this really meant was that Sarah and I got to hang out together a lot. I didn't mind one bit, because she was a serious smoocher who never shied away from my licks (just as I didn't from her kisses). She had started out as a set production assistant on movies such as *The Matrix Reloaded* before she branched into animal training for TV and film. She owned a handsome collie-retriever mix named Kuma, and she was a natural when it came to coaching or 'wrangling', as it's sometimes called in the industry.

Allowing my understudies
a taste of stardom.

As if I needed to be wrangled!

Sarah's company for studio-trained animals was one of the most respected in Hollywood. She offered studios everything from spiders to snakes, llamas to lovebirds, bears to bulldogs, tortoises to tabbies. Neither of us knew it back then, but I was about to become one of her most bankable clients.

Omar took Dash and me through our paces, as we showed off our most photogenic behaviours. He then talked Sarah through some of the cues he used most frequently and warned her of our weaknesses.

'Dash is easily distracted and doesn't have much experience yet,' he told her. 'Uggie has a thing about parrots, squirrels, and occasionally cats. He is also extremely greedy and, left to his own devices, could become a world-class eating machine. So you need to keep him strictly on his treats and well away from the catering truck.'

Spoilsport.

Sarah laughed and told him not to worry, but I could tell Dad was anxious. He rarely spent time away from me, and hardly ever on a job. Knowing that he was watching my every scene, ready to guide me through my stunts, helped me enjoy the moment and give it my best shot. Neither of us knew how things would really go, if he weren't around.

The next issue was whether or not I would get along with my co-star, Jean Dujardin, who was being flown from Paris to meet me. The plan was for us to spend an initial three days together in the big white house that had been rented for him in the Hollywood Hills. We'd then have a couple of weeks getting to know each other better, before filming began.

It is always important for a human to feel completely comfortable in the presence of a canine co-star and vice versa. That way, every glance between them comes across as natural. I shan't name names, but in one movie I was in, the so-called 'star' not only took no interest in getting to know me at all, he objected to having to carry pieces of sausage in his pocket for me (which is a bit like the accounts department objecting that they'd have to carry cash).

He'd turn up sullenly on set, grab my leash, pretty much ignore everything Omar had to say, and just expect me to do my thing for little or no reward. He never once patted me or even looked me in the eye. That guy must have been made of stone. How else could he have resisted me?

Omar knew that I was uncomfortable around someone who can only have been a cat lover, but he kept me focused, and I remained true to my art. It was, however, a joyless (and largely sausage-less) experience, and one neither of us wished to repeat.

'I should warn you,' one of the senior production staff told Omar as we prepared to meet the star of *The Artist*, 'Jean Dujardin doesn't own a dog and isn't so familiar with them … but he is looking forward to meeting Uggie and working with him.'

Great. Another pet hater.

I needn't have worried. All the charm Jean exudes on screen is genuine, to the point where I hesitate even to call him an actor. That's how the man with the laughing eyes is – the real deal. And so much fun to be around! He is a true dog person, and we liked each other immediately. We played ball and Frisbee, I showed him how to skateboard, and he chased me around the lush lawns of the mansion like a doting father.

Whenever we took a break to recover from our exercise, I'd sit on his lap, then turn around three times and settle by his feet. Eventually, I'd fall asleep with my head resting on his shoes, twitching as I chased squirrels in my dreams.

Jean was extremely biddable and eager to learn from me. Not surprisingly, I became instantly and utterly devoted to him. He had suave, European charisma exuding from every pore, and I truly believed that just by being in his Gallic presence, some of his star quality would rub off onto me.

The bad news was that he hardly spoke any English, so we had to communicate through an interpreter much of the time. When he did try to speak in a language we could understand, it had a distinctively European twist. I was accustomed to garbled English (I'd lived with Omar for eight years, after all) but this was off the scale. His attempts to repeat Omar's verbal cues (whenever Omar couldn't be close enough to give them to me himself) came out so strangulated that they were barely discernible as human speech.

Thus 'Roll Over' became 'Wool Uther', 'Sit Pretty' morphed into 'Zeet Preeetie', and 'Speak' transmuted to 'Spick'. In the beginning, I hadn't a canine clue what he was talking about, although I did learn to understand him gradually.

The great news was that because *The Artist* was to be a silent movie, there didn't need to be complete silence on set. Omar would be able to call, whistle, and click for my attention, without it ever affecting the audio.

This was going to be fun.

I was perfect for the role of Jack for so many reasons, but after my embarrassment in *Water for Elephants*, I was delighted to realise that silence in a movie had another benefit: in the scenes where I truly had to Method act and fall asleep, I'd be able to snore to my heart's content. There were two scenes where I had to appear to be asleep, when lying on the bed next to Jean when he was recovering after the fire. I have to admit that my acting was so realistic that I snored spectacularly.

Better still, because there would be no dialogue for the humans, they'd have to learn to perform without the luxury of words, for a change. Every actor – animal or human – would only be able to carry the story through actions, expressions, and gestures, just as I had always done.

At last.

This would be the first vehicle for me in which I'd be at no disadvantage to the humans. Silence was a true leveller.

For the humans, I could tell this was going to be a major leap. Although they were relieved not to have any lines to learn, they didn't realise they had an even bigger challenge on their hands. They'd have to figure out how to use their bodies naturally and without exaggeration, like I did. A scene could be stolen by the simple tilt of a head, an almost imperceptible frown, or a slight parting of the lips.

Too much, and it could look like pantomime. Too little, and it might go unnoticed and couldn't be explained with a line from the script.

The director didn't even want his cast to speak any of the lines that came up on the screen between scenes, because he needed them to focus on how they moved and appeared, rather than worry about the text.

Waiting for my co-star
Jean Dujardin.

Perfect.

Just as Jean could teach me something of his language, so I could teach him the art of a silent actor's craft. No matter how the movie turned out, we were going to have a blast making it.

Watch and learn, Frenchy.

Watch and learn.

## OUR PERFECT COMPANIONS
## NEVER HAVE FEWER THAN
## FOUR FEET.
### *Colette*

Filming began in September 2010 in various locations around Los Angeles and was exciting from the get-go. I can't explain it, but every member of the cast and crew picked up on the buzz of what we all knew was a brave new concept. We somehow realised that we were creating movie magic.

The location managers had done a great job in scouting for the right places to film, so they used some of the city's historic theatres such as the Orpheum, along with several beautiful old houses and the Brennan Building (made famous in the movie *Blade Runner*). The rest was shot on the back lots of Warner Bros and Paramount Studios.

Wherever we were shooting, the amount of effort that went into choosing every detail, from the costumes to the camera angles, was incredible, and Monsieur H. was a master at getting us all in the mood. In a black-and-white movie, everything hinges on two things only: the images and the music, so he focused on both with equal passion. He frequently played music on the set, such as Cole Porter, Duke Ellington, and George Gershwin to keep us in era. It blared out of giant speakers and was only switched off when the cameras began to roll, so that we actors could hear his instructions.

With childlike enthusiasm, Monsieur H. also took his cast to watch silent movies. He encouraged us all to find the inspiration for our characters from the Hollywood greats. The humans were urged to read the memoirs and biographies of some of the great silent movie stars, including John Gilbert – on whose character the film was loosely based.

I, of course, had the early canon of Rin Tin Tin to draw from, but, in truth, I made the part my own.

My dear Jean found his greatest inspiration in the life of Douglas Fairbanks Jr, but also claimed to have copied Gene Kelly for his smile, Vittorio Gassman for his movement, and Clark Gable for his moustache. He added, 'And I watched Lassie, who was happy as a dog.'

Grrrrr.

Actor John Goodman, who played a big-time Hollywood producer, said he was inspired by Cecil B. DeMille. Bérénice Bejo (Madame H. in real life), who played Jean's love interest, Peppy Miller, joked that I had a bigger part than her. That changed as soon as everyone saw how fabulous she was on camera, and from then on, her pretty face filled almost every frame. She claimed to have drawn on Greta Garbo and Mary Pickford for her inspiration.

Some of our scenes were actually shot in an incredible *beaux arts* mansion in Fremont Place, Beverly Hills, in which Mary Pickford had lived for a while. It was said to be the place where she began her affair with Douglas Fairbanks Jr, and it thrilled me to think I marked the territory where the actor who played Zorro once stood.

The movie was shot in colour but tinted later. The cameramen used special filters to make the film more monochrome. Every shade of fabric or paint was carefully considered in both colour and black and white, to make sure they came out the right kind of grey in the finished product. Prints and florals were out, and shiny textures and metallics were in (although this hardly bothered me).

Everything from the scenery to the lighting was kept very high contrast or in silhouette, unless it was to portray Jean's career slide when he moved from always being in the spotlight to being shot only in low light or smoky darkness.

Special attention was paid to the costumes. As Jean's fortunes fell in the plot, so his clothes became greyer. By the time he was destitute, he was placed in suits two sizes too big and made to wear weighted shoes, in order to drag his feet.

I managed to drag my paws alongside him, without any need for special props. Acting!

Jean was also only ever filmed going downstairs – never up – to emphasise the same point, while Peppy went upstairs, and her clothes became lighter and brighter, as her career developed and the story progressed.

**In make-up and ready for action
on the set of *The Artist*.**

Incidentally, during the scenes depicting her earliest roles in silent movies, she was listed on the film credits incorrectly as 'Peppi' Miller, which I guess was a way of showing the audience how getting her name right wasn't important for such a lowly star. Similarly, though, I was listed on one of the same credits as 'Uggy' the dog, not even as 'Jack', my official character name.

Although my name was corrected in the final credits, in a few countries where the movie was shown (especially France), I became forever known as 'Uggy'.

Just like the other stars, I spent a lot of time in hair and make-up most days. Unlike them, I had my very own 'animal colourist', Rose Ordile, who used vegetable dyes to colour in my fur where necessary and keep me in high contrast. Because Dash and Dude had been hired, in case I was injured or got sick, Dude and I underwent the daily indignity of having Dash's asymmetrical neck markings painted onto our perfect coats, for continuity purposes.

I didn't complain, but I felt it was a complete waste of time that detracted from my natural good looks.

Needless to say, Dash was only ever used in a few seconds of one shot at the beginning of the movie, when George Valentin walks away from the camera, along a darkened tunnel, and Dash trots alongside him. It was a scene I'd have taken in my stride, but Dad wanted to test Dash out, to see if he would perform under pressure. He did all right, and I'm happy to give credit where credit is due, but I always felt that there was too much spring in his step.

Dude featured minimally, as well, in a scene where Penelope Ann Miller (playing George's unhappy wife) threw a newspaper at George, while I was sitting next to him on a couch. Now, I'm a real easygoing kind of a guy. I get along with everyone and have rarely, if ever, been known to respond aggressively to anyone other than cats, goats, squirrels, parrots, or zebras. But when Penelope hurled that paper at my beloved Jean – and made me flinch in a reflex – I didn't like it one little bit.

As an emotional actor, I was cursed with a happy puppy-hood. I had never been abused. No one had ever thrown a thing at me. I didn't know how to respond, other than defensively.

Take two had me growling, and by take five, I was snapping at the darned newspaper. I think Penelope was worried I might snap at her. In came Dude, a former pound dog twice rejected by previous humans and probably mistreated. All he did when that paper was thrown at him was duck slightly and jump off the seat.

I was happy to allow him his moment of fame.

In spite of those two substitutions, I was firing on all cylin-ders while making that movie. I had such a ball throughout, and I was treated as an equal player from the start. Admittedly, the days were long and intense, especially for someone approaching 60 in human years, but I was extremely well looked after. Even when I was on set for up to 18 hours a day, Omar and Sarah made sure I had plenty of rest in my trailer between shoots.

The hardest part for me was responding to the 'Go With' cue in a busy environment, such as a crowd or noisy street, with vintage cars whizzing past. One of the most challenging scenes was the sequence early on, in which Jean and I emerged from his latest film premiere and out onto a street packed with 200 or so extras playing adoring fans and press photographers.

With so many people in the frame, there could be no acting coaches close at hand. Jean had to work with me by himself, while remembering to hit his own marks. My role was to stay with him throughout, keep in shot, sniff for sausages, watch for cues, and all the while try to remain calm in a sea of excitable legs.

It was a long scene to have to do multiple times and land on the same mark from multiple angles, but between us, we almost always nailed it, mainly because Sarah and I had prepped the heck out of that scene. To me, it was a bit like memorising lines; I just had to keep at it, until I got it right.

Sarah certainly seemed pleased with my work, and Dad never stopped congratulating me. 'You're doing such a great job, buddy!' he'd tell me, rubbing me in that spot that makes my back leg go all jiggery. Or he'd cry, 'You nailed that scene, Ugg!' or 'That was awesome, boy!' One time, he ran up to me after another successful take and told me tearfully, 'You're so smart, Uggie, sometimes I don't even believe you're a dog!'

High praise indeed.

I have to say I was pretty pleased with him, too. We'd worked together seamlessly for eight years, and we had developed a uniquely collaborative relationship that allowed me to take all my emotional cues from him. Trust, of course, played a huge part, but mostly it was love – oh, and my edible pay cheques.

Even Monsieur H., who admitted that he'd only added a dog to the movie originally for a little light relief, quickly realised how integral my role was to become. 'Uggie was a star,' he marvelled later. 'It was a pleasure to work with such a pro. He became very important in the movie – much more than I had expected when I wrote the script. To me, it was just fun to have a dog, because it changed the profile of the main character, and it was very period.

'But, when we started filming, everyone so loved Uggie that he almost stole the show, and I tried to figure out why that was. Then I got it – the main character George is not so sympathetic, and he makes a lot of mistakes, but the dog follows him, whatever happens. People trust the dog, so you begin to accept the main character because of the dog.'

*Très vrai, Monsieur.* How true.

**26**

IF A DOG WILL NOT COME TO YOU
AFTER HAVING LOOKED YOU IN THE
FACE, YOU SHOULD GO HOME AND
EXAMINE YOUR CONSCIENCE.
*Woodrow Wilson*

I think I speak for all my fellow cast members when I say in tribute to Monsieur H. that, under his direction, *The Artist* allowed me to be the best actor I could possibly be. With my instinctive intelligence, enthusiasm, and dogged work ethic, I was able to give him what he wanted, and so much more.

My character, 'Jack', was tender and uncomplicated, cute, funny, and brave. Not only was I in almost every scene (and featured in a huge oil painting on the wall of George's house), I was also allowed to showcase my capacity for humour and poignancy. The arc of Jack's story was just as much of an emotional journey as his master's. No matter how low George's fortunes sank, Jack remained a loyal and loving companion – and the last friend he had left in the world.

Talk about pathos.

There was one scene where George had just watched a test for the first talking picture, and he laughed at it derisively. I looked up and barked my views on the matter in a way that said it all, as far as I was concerned.

Captured in oils on the
set of *The Artist.*

Rather unnecessarily, in my opinion, George's words were then flashed up on the screen: 'If only he could talk!'

Speak for yourself, Monsieur.

On the set of that movie, grown men wept in certain scenes when they saw how Jean and I interacted. They had no dialogue to listen to; they just saw us working together so devotedly that they couldn't help but be touched by our connection.

The script also gave me my first chance to be a hero. From the moment I appeared as a giant shadow on a wall within three minutes of the movie starting, I was a saviour and as much a part of the drama as George. In the persona of my silent-movie character, I began by squeezing through the bars of the jail in which my master was being held, to lick him awake (helped by a little melted butter, I have to admit).

To anyone who has never worked with a director and cinematographer, it may have looked like a simple shot. Those with experience will know that nothing is simple in the movies. To begin with, they wanted me to wriggle through the second and third bar from the left, so Sarah let me go, and Omar enticed me through those two bars in repeated takes. He stood just below the window, out of view, and I had to leap down into his arms. We did it many times, and we both thought I'd done a good job.

Then the director looked at how the scene was shot through the playback viewer, and after much consultation, he decided that my shadow would look bigger and better if I squeezed through the wall and the first bar instead. That took a lot of getting used to, when I had just been 'patterned' (to use a technical term) to go through the other two bars. It took me a while to understand the new direction, but we got there in the end (with a little help from a trail of sausage scent), and I have to admit, my shadow never looked better.

In the movie's most dramatic scene, I had a leading role that was vital to the plot. In surely my greatest moment, I saved a suicidal George from a blazing house. We shot the fire scene over several days, and in a couple of different locations. Sarah worked on a lot of the exterior shots, too. Certain scenes required both of my trainers, such as the one in which I was running to summon the police officer.

In one take, Sarah rode off on a golf buggy calling me to follow. But the buggy was too slow, so they had to reshoot the whole running scene. On another take, she ran ahead of me on foot and was really energetic as she let me chase after her. Omar then switched from a buggy to a bicycle, and I happily chased after him, eager to get my treat. We went so fast, in fact, that Dad almost ran over a couple of the extras dawdling on the sidewalk.

When Monsieur H. shouted 'Action!' (a cue I knew only too well), I also had to run inside the smoky 'house' and search for Jean. Behind the camera and sitting astride the smoke machine (to the point that she almost suffocated), Sarah was calling me loudly and squeezing a few of my favourite squeaky toys, in order to be heard above all the real-life din. Even though I knew the fire had been set deliberately and that there were firefighters on standby, in case it got out of control, there were still real flames and smoke so thick all around me that I couldn't see.

The room was very hot, and the drama intense, as the flames licked higher and higher. Every fibre of my canine being urged me to flee a place of such danger, and it took several takes to get it right. With either Sarah or Omar always within earshot calling their encouragement, I managed to do all that was expected of me and more.

Lassie? Go home …

Jean taught me so much: how to work with the camera and use my body to express myself. He collaborated with me as an actor, never worked against me, and didn't once cut me off or push me out of the frame. He was a true gentleman and allowed me my many moments in the spotlight.

As he said later, 'Uggie's a smart fellow! He's a great actor, he can steal a scene, no problem. Working with him was very simple … The only problem was keeping bits of sausage in your pocket all day long … Some days, I felt like I was just a great big sausage.'

As if that were a bad thing!

When he was brought out of the burning house and laid on the lawn, for example, he did indeed have small pieces of hot dog hidden in every pocket. I sniffed all around him, following the heady scent, but I still managed to appear deeply concerned for my master. My whiskers must have tickled his face once or twice, as there were a couple of takes in which he got the giggles.

But mostly he let me play my part, until Monsieur H. was happy and shouted my second favourite word: 'Cut!'

Discussing my fees with my *Artist*
co-star John Goodman.

In one of my most talked-about scenes, where Jean lifted me onto the breakfast table, it was me that led the way. If you watch that again carefully, you will see that it was *him* mimicking *my* actions, rather than the other way around. It is only when I stayed with my head tucked under my leg that he took over and dipped the end of his nose in his cream. That was my cue to lift my head and lick it off.

Ours was truly a movie-making partnership.

Jean said afterwards, 'I can't speak American dog very well, so there was a lot of improvisation with Uggie ... Sometimes I followed him, sometimes he followed me.'

My payment in treats became a bit of an issue on set, I can now reveal. Some of my fellow actors (who can't be named) threatened to sack their agents and book mine instead.

'How come Uggie's the only one around here who gets a sausage each time he does something right?' they complained bitterly.

Even Jean became a little disgruntled. 'He had a lot of massages and hot dogs and bones, and we didn't have those treats,' he moaned later.

The traditional response of 'Call the union!' didn't work with me, because I didn't have to belong to one. The closest I got to it was the various animal welfare unions that Omar was signed up to, including the American Humane Association, but they were hardly going to take up the case of a few extras.

Oops ... Pavlovian slip.

## TO ERR IS HUMAN,
## TO FORGIVE, CANINE.
### *Unknown*

Not that everything went smoothly every day on the set of *The Artist*. During weeks and weeks of filming, everyone made mistakes, especially when they were tired or had too much to think about. Like me, my co-star Jean had a wonderful knack for keeping things light, and his whimsical expressions or sudden grins were always welcome icebreakers.

Bérénice had her moments, too, and her tennis playing in one scene proved her game to be about as skilled as mine (we lost count of the takes on that one). She was also prone to sudden fits of the giggles during some of her scenes with Jean, usually because he said something funny or was making a face. It took them five months of practice to learn their final dance sequence (17 takes!), and the gaffes in that seemed relentless. Jean was a master at playing the fool, and Bérénice slipped on the polished floor.

To his credit, Monsieur H. didn't seem to mind at all, and he often laughed as he reminded us to 'Have fun!'

I am proud to say that I was rarely a disappointment to the director, cast, or crew. If we ever had to go again, it was generally because of someone else's blooper. Right on cue, I barked vociferously and from my diaphragm (just as Omar had taught me), as Jean sank into movie quicksand. I stuck by him in speeding automobiles and in rocking biplanes.

If I had any faults, it was that I would sometimes pre-empt my cue a few seconds before the right moment. I knew what I had to do, and I guess I was just too keen to do it. I also had a bit of trouble concealing my tremor, especially when I was tired. It didn't usually affect me so much when I was working, because my body is so wired for action, but there is one scene in which it can clearly be seen.

George has moved from his big house to a crummy apartment, and I am sitting, looking up at him, full of love. My front legs are quivering visibly, but I think it adds to the drama and emotion of the new situation Jack finds himself in. We actors can only work with what we have, right?

My worst moments came when Omar had to leave the set. He had no choice but to get on a plane with Jumpy, Popeye, Gordo, and Julio, and fly to Venezuela for *The Incredible Dogs Show*.

'Stay focused,' he told me, staring deeply into my eyes before he left. 'Do as Sarah says, and be a good boy, okay buddy?'

I was secretly anxious about him leaving, but to reassure him, I gave his face a good long lick and then went to work on his ears. He needed to look his best in Caracas, after all.

Once he was no longer in my peripheral vision offering daily reassurance, though, I'm afraid I sometimes lost concentration and fell apart. It was much tougher to work without my own personal trainer than I'd ever thought. All that I knew, I'd learned from him. Not having him with me felt like I was missing a paw.

That kind of intense co-dependency between artist and coach happens all the time. It was evocatively portrayed in *My Week with Marilyn*, with Michelle Williams as Marilyn Monroe and Zoë Wanamaker as her coach, Paula Strasberg. As that other great coach, Stella Adler, once said: 'The actor cannot afford to look only to his own life for all his material, nor pull strictly from his own experience to find his acting choices and feelings.'

Too true.

What happened next can best be described as Blooper-Gate. I have to confess to having a slightly mischievous streak, which is something that was bred into me, I guess. It is the reason we are occasionally known as 'Jack Russell Terrorists'. With Omar away from the set, the chance to be naughty presented itself to me, and on a few occasions, I simply couldn't resist.

Sarah is an excellent wrangler, at the top of her profession, and one of the few people Omar would entrust with my care. But no amount of training and experience will help if an actor like me develops an impish impulse or two, and that is precisely what happened.

If I'd hoped that any of my rebellious moments might have been overlooked, I was very much mistaken, though. The minute the movie became a success, all those scenes were painstakingly pieced together and included on a blooper reel released on YouTube. My shame has been seen by thousands. Worse than that, though; it has been seen by Omar. I felt as if I'd let him down.

What I would say in my defence is that the out-takes only go to show how professional I was the rest of the time, and how hard it is for an actor always to remain focused – especially without his mentor to guide him.

In one of the first scenes on the blooper reel, Jean opened the door of a darkened cinema and expected me to follow him out – a move I would normally follow to the letter with the cue 'Go With'. For some reason, I either didn't hear Sarah or I was confused in the darkness, so I headed towards her, instead. She called out to me to stop, so I did, and then I looked back at Jean, who gesticulated wildly for me to go with him. Puzzled as to what to do, I stood waiting for clearer instructions, until Jean feigned exasperation with me and threw his hat onto the floor. Everyone fell about.

I did something similar during a scene in which Jean was on stage in front of a huge audience of dolled-up extras, and he called me on from his right. Sarah was standing in the wings to his left so I ran straight past my new French *ami* instead of stopping as I was supposed to. Bless him, he just grinned and shrugged at the laughing crowd.

Later, on the same stage, Jean made as if to shoot me with his finger, but he didn't do it quite the same way as Omar did, and I wasn't sure I'd seen it right. Waiting for further cues, I sat patiently staring up at him. Smiling, Jean took his imaginary gun and pretended to shoot himself instead.

On a later take, when I didn't respond again to the 'Bang!' cue, Jean did something truly spontaneous. He pretended to toss away his finger gun and pull out a much larger weapon from inside his tuxedo before screwing a silencer onto it so as to do the job properly. What a comedian! Needless to say, everybody cracked up.

I only have one complaint about my whole extraordinary experience of starring in *The Artist*. As so often happens in an actor's career, my best scene really did end up on the cutting-room floor. Fortunately, Omar was back, so he did at least get to see it.

What I considered to be my award-winning moment came towards the end of the movie, when Jean had to put a pistol in his mouth, as if intending to kill himself. I was supposed to sit at his feet, barking my concern for my beloved master. Jean played his part so brilliantly, though, and came across as such a desperate man, that he actually began to tremble a little as he brought the weapon to his mouth.

Totally engrossed in my role and picking up on his emotion, I engaged with him completely and feared that something bad might happen to the human with whom I'd formed such a strong bond. (It isn't always easy for an actor like me to distinguish between life and art.)

Ignoring any cues, I responded viscerally to what I suddenly perceived as a threat to dear Jean. I jumped off my mark, leapt up onto his lap and tried to pull the pistol out of his hand with my teeth.

No acting required.

For once, Jean didn't smile. He just looked at me with such love and admiration; I knew he shared my pain.

As Omar explained later, 'When Uggie put his mouth on Jean's hand and started pulling it, we were so stunned. I think Uggie felt he was in danger and was trying to stop him hurting himself. He wasn't told to do that.'

Outside the set, Sarah was watching on a monitor and said everyone around her was moved. 'I cried like an idiot,' she said. 'Uggie was acting in the moment. He was responding to the actor in an emotional sense. I think that's a form of acting that was incredible to see. I don't know why they didn't use that take. It was amazing.'

Omar asked Monsieur H. about that later and the director said that when they revisited the scene it was almost too much; too emotional. They loved it, but it wasn't exactly what they wanted.

And so, my finest theatrical hour was never saved for cinematic posterity. I console myself with the fact that I know what I did that day, and so do those closest to me.

That, folks, is show biz.

## IF YOU TOOK ACTING AWAY FROM ME,
## I'D STOP BREATHING.
### *Ingrid Bergman*

Filming finished in November 2010, and everyone was sorry that it had come to an end. The rapport between cast and crew had been remarkable, and there were genuine tears of sadness at the wrap party.

I was especially sad to be parting from Jean Dujardin, a human surpassing most others and, I might even say, on a par with Omar when it came to his understanding of the canine mind.

*Au revoir, mon ami!*

After such an intense experience – and because of my recently diagnosed condition – I acted on medical advice and took a sabbatical. Omar insisted that I chill out while some of the younger guys in the pack put their shoulders to the wheel of breadwinning. I missed the work, but decided not to argue.

In a loose-fitting casual collar, I spent most of my time lounging by the pool or in front of the TV. Dad cosseted me constantly and would sometimes join me to watch an action movie or his favourite late-night talk-show host Jay Leno (who always reminds me of a husky, for some reason).

When I wasn't relaxing, I made sure to keep on top of my fitness, because I've seen what happens to those actors who take a break from the business (and yes, I'm talking about you, Dude).

Between takes with Bérénice,
Jean, Omar, and Monsieur H.

After some squirrel chasing, swimming, and maybe a bit of light skateboarding, I would occasionally play with Flash the turtle – not that I think she'd call it playing. Whenever Omar would let her out of her tank to stretch her legs, I'd take an almost devilish delight in watching her for a while before flipping her over onto her back with my paw. Her little legs would rotate like clockwork (great exercise, I always thought) as she tried to right herself. Then, just when she started to tire, I'd flip her back over again and watch her try to make her getaway.

I blame this unusually sadistic trait on Gizmo, the cat. Although Gizmo had gone to that great velvet cushion in the sky, he'd left me with a legacy of feline indifference that I couldn't quite shake. If cats were so cool (and everyone agreed they were), then maybe their coolness came out of their tyranny to smaller creatures?

There was, you see, an inner Uggie that desperately wanted to be cool. Not cute, not adorable, not even lovable, but Clooney-cool. I wanted a house on a lake and to look terrific even though my fur was going grey. I wanted men and women to fawn over me and hang on my every woof.

For all I knew, George flipped turtles at home too, just to stay on top.

Luckily for Flash, I quickly grew bored with the game and abandoned it after a few minutes – always making sure to flip her right-side up as I went. My heart wasn't in cruelty. I guess I'd just have to accept myself for who I was – the most adorable dog on the planet.

Feeling better, I sat back and watched some favourite movies, including *Turner & Hooch*, *Beethoven* (for which they used three canines, including a she-dog), *Homeward Bound: The Incredible Journey*, and *Best in Show*. I surfed the cable networks but was disappointed by the scarcity of canines in *Dog the Bounty Hunter* and, as always, winced at the typecast demonisation of larger dogs.

When are you guys going to figure out that Rottweilers are really big pussycats?

Keeping my paws on the Hollywood pulse, I quickly gathered from *E! News* that *The Artist* was being widely talked about, having previously been considered the quirky art-house underdog. There was a buzz about how good our film was going to be.

For a silent movie, it was starting to make some serious noise.

The world premiere was to be at the Cannes Film Festival in May 2011, and when Omar told me that there was a chance we might get to go, I could hardly believe it. Aside from touring Latin America with *The Incredible Dogs Show*, I'd hardly been out of the United States and never to Europe. Cannes wasn't just Europe; it was in the south of France – a place synonymous with wealth and glamour, poodles, Chihuahuas, and pugs.

In short, a place where rich people favoured small dogs. What wasn't to like?

Better still, I'd also heard that Cannes had the most enticing *fin-de-siècle* lampposts. I could hardly wait to start sending p-mail!

I might even be able to chill out on the beach where Brigitte Bardot had been photographed in her prime. What a heroine to rescue dogs that shaggy-haired human was! BB's Foundation for the Welfare and Protection of Animals had saved countless dogs, as well as dolphins, cats, horses, bears, tigers, elephants, rhinos, and seals from death. Like most males of a certain age, I longed to meet her and lick her face in heartfelt appreciation.

When we heard that the American movie mogul Harvey Weinstein had snapped up global distribution rights to *The Artist* after being invited to a private screening, we knew we were really onto something. This meant that our humble 100-minute picture wouldn't only be shown in Europe, but around the world.

Omar needn't have worried about getting hold of a copy, after all.

My handsomely hirsute face, with its distinguished flecks of grey, would appear internationally and on the big screen. I'd be towering 20 feet above audiences and in high definition in places as far afield as New York and Rome, London and Beijing, Paris and Tokyo. I tried not to worry that my nose might look too big in HD.

As is often the way of things in show biz, good news was tempered by bad. My hoped-for trip to Cannes didn't happen. The decision about my going or not had been left to the last minute, and there wasn't enough time left to organise my complicated canine travel requirements.

*Zut alors!*

What did I care? The boulevards would have been hot and crowded, especially the famous Promenade de la Croisette along the seafront. There'd have been no privacy thanks to all the paparazzi, and the endless photo calls and interviews would have been a formidable undertaking for an actor of my years.

Brigitte, alas, would have to wait.

Most of my fellow co-stars on *The Artist* went in my place and did a wonderful job promoting our movie. I was delighted when dear Jean was voted Best (Human) Actor. In spite of my bravest terrier face, I'd have liked to have been there to congratulate him in person, doggone it.

Even more galling was that I was unable to collect the coveted Palm Dog award, given to me by the international film critics for Best Performance by a Canine. '[Uggie] was light, lovable, plain fun and funny,' announced the judges. A play on the Palme d'Or (the festival's highest honour), the Palm Dog prize was the fabulous leather collar that was to become my favourite.

Previous recipients in the award's 11-year history included Mops in *Marie Antoinette*, Bruno in *The Cave of the Yellow Dog*, and Boss in *Tamara Drewe*. I tried to overlook that the critics had also awarded it to Moses in *Dogville* (represented by a chalk outline through most of that movie) and Dug, a *cartoon* dog from *Up* (which really got my hackles *up*).

Puh-leeze.

The Palm Dog award was collected on my behalf by a French Jack Russell named Apple, or presumably Pomme? The judges felt that her breed qualified her for the substitution alone, and then her hair-salon owner apparently suggested that she was my pen pal. One downside of the fame game is that there will always be those who will claim to know you or have some kind of spurious connection to you.

The idea that I would be a pen pal with Apple, whoever she was, was plainly ridiculous. Julio had been handling all my correspondence for some years, and he'd never respond without my express permission.

Celebrating my Palm Dog award
in Beverly Hills.

## A DOG HAS LOTS OF FRIENDS BECAUSE
## HE WAGS HIS TAIL AND NOT HIS TONGUE.
### *Anonymous*

Having set tongues and tails wagging on the Croisette and beyond, every member of the cast – including me – was enlisted for a whirlwind publicity tour to help promote the movie for the next round of awards.

Between us, we attended scores of guild screenings and Q&A sessions, as well as just about every major media event on the awards-season circuit. In what proved to be a fantastically exciting but physically exhausting few months, I performed time and again for photographers.

I also still had my day job, so I had to fly to South Africa to star in the Savanna dry cider commercial. Dash was my understudy again, so he came along, too (which at least meant I had some company in the hold). Together, we spent several days under hot lights perfecting what would become a classic commercial in its genre.

The shoot was in a famous bar in Johannesburg called the Radium Beer Hall, which was once an illegal speakeasy. In the storyline of the commercial, a man sat by himself at a long wooden bar drinking from a bottle of the famous-brand cider. Suddenly, I skateboarded past him – not once, but three times.

The first time I did it normally, the second time I added a turn-around in the middle, and finally I went up on my back legs and pushed myself along.

All Dash had to do was sit on his skateboard at the end of the bar whimpering as if he wanted to join in.

The customer and the barman watched me pass up and down in silence and then the customer asked the barman, 'Are those Jack Russells?'

Deadpan, and polishing a glass, the barman replied, 'No, they're mine.'

The commercial might look effortless, but so much practice went into getting it right. The narrow and highly polished bar counter was faithfully reproduced in a studio in Los Angeles – with exactly the same height and dimensions – so that I could rehearse my moves for weeks, skateboarding up and down without risk of falling off and hurting myself.

Then, when we arrived in South Africa, I had to prove to the 30-plus crew, including the directors, marketing staff, and producers, that I could perform on cue. No pressure, then. The strange thing for Omar and me after *The Artist* was that he could no longer vocalise my cues or talk me through a take. He had to revert back to our old system of sign language and encouraging expressions. Thankfully, it all went according to plan, and everyone seemed pleased, especially Dad. I think he must have smooched me all the way back to the airport.

There was little time to rest before we were off again – this time to South America to start touring with *The Incredible Dogs Show*. As well as showing me off, Dad decided to take the amazingly talented Jumpy, Julio, and Gordo to show off their skateboarding and agility skills. We all flew to Mexico and arrived at the airport very early one morning, but then the problems began.

I could smell trouble the moment we landed and barked my concern to Omar through the bars of my crate, but he was tired and too busy dealing with paperwork to listen.

'You can only bring two dogs into the country per person,' a stony-faced customs official suddenly told him.

'But I've been all over the world with more than two dogs,' he cried. 'Nobody told me about this and I have four dogs with me!'

'You must pay a fine for one extra, but the fourth animal will have to be held in our warehouse until you have been to the relevant departments and got the correct paperwork.'

'Warehouse?' Omar asked, suspiciously. 'What is that and where?'

'It's a depot for seized goods, about a mile away.'

I barked my mistrust and scratched furiously at the door of my crate. Omar looked down at me this time and sensed my fear, just as I could smell his.

'Well, how long will this paperwork take?'

The official shrugged. 'A few hours, maybe more. You'll have to wait for the office to open first.'

Omar's face fell. Now I could smell anger. He hated the idea of parting company with any one of us, even for a short period of time. Scratching his head, he stared down at the four of us looking dolefully up at him from our doggy crates and wondered what he should do.

'You must decide which one to leave,' he was told. 'And quickly.'

Julio and Gordo were very popular breeds in South America, and Omar feared they'd be the most likely to be stolen. Jumpy was the youngest and the least unusual as a mixed-breed Border collie. Omar had never been able to find him a double, though, in spite of hours trawling the Internet. I was the eldest and a movie star; but he did have two doubles for me. Even though I couldn't bear to let Omar out of my sight, I'd have happily sacrificed myself for my brothers, and I told him so, but still he didn't listen.

Dad said later that it was one of the toughest decisions he'd ever had to make in his life. 'It was like choosing which of my own children to send to prison.' With a heavy heart, he finally picked sweet Jumpy for the warehouse.

Having paid the fine for a third dog and transported us to the hotel he had booked in the city, he hurried back to the airport to begin the complicated paper trail required to release Jumpy. To his enormous dismay, it took far longer than he'd been told, and he kept having to dash from one office to the other to get yet another form filled in or a different section stamped.

'It was my worst nightmare,' he said later. 'The hours passed, and I was so worried about Jumpy. I knew he'd be anxious and unable to exercise or relieve himself.'

As the day drew to an end, and the hour loomed when he knew the warehouse would close for the night, Omar still didn't have the necessary documentation, so he panicked. He got in his hire car and drove out to the depot where he persuaded the guards to allow him at least to let Jumpy out for a short walk and give him some food and water.

'He was so pleased to see me and thought I'd come to take him away. The warehouse was huge and full of everything from household items to pets, including lizards and cats. The men there didn't appear to care. I thought an animal might die in there, and they wouldn't even notice. It was terrible having to put Jumpy back in his crate for the night and say goodbye.'

Not one of us slept that night; we paced up and down in our hotel room, worrying about dear Jumpy. Omar was beside himself and didn't even undress; he wanted to be up and out early to chase up the further documentation.

The following day proved to be just as much of a headache for him, though. In desperation, he called a friend named Cathy who, he remembered, had had a similar problem with a dog in Mexico a few years earlier.

'Oh my God, Omar. You have to get Jumpy out of there!' she told him long-distance. 'They kept my dog for a week, even though I went there every day, crying and pleading, but they wouldn't release him.'

Sweating, and with time running out on the second day, Omar eventually managed to convince the authorities that Jumpy was no threat. It was only at the eleventh hour, and as the last guard left at the warehouse was about to close the gates for the night, that he was able to spring his beloved Border collie mix back to the hotel.

Poor Jumpy. When he came running into that room to see us, he was seriously spooked. We could all smell his angst. Omar, too, was badly shaken. We licked them both all over by way of mutual reassurance and agreed that we'd never put any one of us through anything like that again. We have not been back to Mexico since.

**30**

## AN OUNCE OF BEHAVIOUR IS
## WORTH A POUND OF WORDS.
### *Sanford Meisner*

No sooner were we home than the media frenzy for *The Artist* resumed. I made appearance after appearance: on TV and radio shows, at charity events, and in interviews with print journalists. I was a big hit.

One interviewer even said that I had an 'adorable expression and limpid eyes, the colour of stewed tea'.

Stewed tea?

Move over, Brad Pitt, these are some real puppy-dog eyes!

There is nothing like getting out there among the fans, and I enjoyed meeting all those who really seemed to love our movie. It was humbling to see how connected people felt to my character, and it was extraordinary to realise that they felt as if they knew me personally. I guess humans find it difficult to distinguish life from art too, sometimes.

As ever, Omar let everyone pat and kiss me as much as they wanted, and I learned to adopt a kind of doggy smile for the photographs. I also thanked Mercy privately every day for having my teeth whitened. As she so rightly predicted, that stuff really matters when you're in front of a hundred flash bulbs.

Our hard work began to pay off, because by November 2011, not only was the movie a favourite for all the major awards, but something else rather wonderful happened. A wise and generous human named S. T. VanAirsdale, an editor at the website Movieline, set up a 'Consider Uggie' campaign on Facebook and Twitter, urging the Academy of Motion Picture Arts and Sciences to present me with a special animal Oscar for Best Supporting Actor.

He wrote, 'Uggie inhabits a character and emotional range as evocative as any of his human co-stars … He handily outperforms Leo (DiCaprio) in *J. Edgar*, though might not measure up to Clooney's work in *The Descendants*.'

He added, 'Retrograde union and Academy rules may prohibit a nomination for Uggie in categories historically reserved for humans, but it's time for critics and awards bodies such as the Golden Globes to take a good, hard look into Uggie's huge eyes and huger talent and reverse the discriminatory trend that prohibits recognition of this level of animal artistry.'

Humblingly, his was not a lone voice in the wilderness. Lou Lumenick, the *New York Post* film critic who'd similarly tried to convince the New York Film Critics Circle to give me a special award, added, 'Uggie gives the best performance, human or animal, in any film I've seen this year.' Roger Friedman at Showbiz411 added that I gave the year's 'most consistent and memorable performance', and would win Best Supporting Actor 'if I and PETA could say anything about it'.

The Facebook and Twitter campaigns quickly amassed more than 20,000 followers, and before I knew it I had my own pages on each of the popular social networking sites (although I left their management largely to Omar and Mercy).

Dad was puffed up like one of his performing pigeons, he was so proud. Whenever anybody asked him if I deserved an Oscar, he let them have it. 'I think it's about time that a dog was recognised, and it is great that people are pushing for it.' He'd insist, 'Uggie does real acting; he is not just following instructions or hoping for sausages. He has been doing this for nine years. He never has a leash on, and he remains with the actor at all times. Cars go by and he is never hit. He is not afraid of fire, smoke, or any commotion, and does so many things right on the money. He has experience and training and is a real actor – I don't care what anyone says.'

We must have been doing something right, because in December 2011, *The Artist* won the New York Film Critics Circle Award for Best Picture. With that success under my collar, I grabbed my pet passport (a European requirement), packed my best leash, and flew off with Omar in January for nine days of media promotion in London, England.

Although I loathed the 11-hour journey in the hold (never again!), my ancestral home of Great Britain was all I'd hoped it would be and more. I was very surprised that it wasn't rainy or foggy like in all the American movies. In fact, it was warmer than LA. I was also disappointed not to meet any of the Queen's corgis, but I did wave a paw as we passed Buckingham Palace on our way to a special charity screening of our movie in the West End, in aid of the Dogs Trust.

I stayed in a trendy five-star hotel and travelled all over town in a chauffeur-driven Jaguar, causing quite a stir wherever I went. Even though I was a seasoned pro, I still fed off the energy and excitement people had for me and played to the gallery every time. The eminent British newspaper *The Guardian* invited me to its offices and created a special black-and-white video of my visit, which quickly went viral.

The *Daily Mail* wasn't quite so charitable. One reporter rather unkindly said that I had 'sausage breath' and looked older in the flesh. Omar responded, 'Well, he did wear a little bit of make-up in the film … a little bit of darkening around the eye. A little bit to hide his grey. You see, Uggie is nearly 10. He's not a kid any more. What has happened to him recently has been fantastic, but I wish it had happened earlier. It would have been electric.'

I met a lady called Gabby Logan and appeared on her live radio show, which was fun because I got to sit (and snooze) on a velvet cushion. I had lunch at a fancy restaurant, where Omar fed me the finest raw tuna inbetween consecutive media interviews. (I asked to take my leftovers home in a 'manny bag'.)

On 6 January, I appeared on the most popular TV chat show in the UK, hosted by a very funny fellow named Graham

Norton. There were a couple of other guests, including a singer called Noel Gallagher, and a fellow thespian named Gerard Butler, but I gave them each a courtesy lick and then focused on my moment in the spotlight.

Mr Norton and I were destined to get along, as he was the master of a Labradoodle called Bailey and a rescue mutt named Madge. I loved his edgy humour and twinkling smile and thought he seemed far more interested in me skateboarding than anything his other guests had to say.

I like that in a human.

Showcasing my talents on
*The Graham Norton Show.*

I learned that Joey, the equine star of *War Horse*, was also in town for the premiere of his movie – a rival for ours at the awards. I didn't mind horses so much, but they were a bit too similar to zebras for my liking, so I kept well away.

Omar and I flew back across the pond (seriously, the hold, again?), just missing the British Academy of Film and Television Awards in London on 12 February. That was a pity, because *The Artist* was named Best Film and won six other awards. We were on a roll.

Monsieur H. went up on stage and told the people of Britain, 'This is a good day!' When it was Jean Dujardin's turn, he announced, 'I love your country!' and told the director, 'This is your fault! What have you done to me?' He said he was proud to be recognised by his peers in the nation that had produced Sir Laurence Olivier, William Webb Ellis (the inventor of a human ball game called rugby), and Benny Hill.

Although there had been a campaign in England to get me nominated, too, BAFTA officials decided that I lacked the 'essential attribute of being a human' and was therefore not qualified. A spokesman added, 'Uggie is not a human being and his unique motivation as an actor is sausages.'

Obviously! Have they tried eating cash?

I thought Omar's response said it all: 'People say that dogs in films are just doing what they are told. But an actor is just following the director's orders. They say that a dog is only working for sausages, but an actor is only doing it for his paycheck.'

*Touché.*

We returned to LA for the 69th annual Golden Globes awards ceremony on 15 January 2012, at the Beverly Hilton Hotel. I'd hardly recovered from jet lag before I was back in a bow tie, my nails buffed and my fur groomed, ready for yet another night on the red carpet.

The evening was made all the more exciting by the news that *The Artist* had just won Best Picture and Best Actress at the French equivalent of the Golden Globes, the Lumière Awards.

*Vive la France!*

I was never really fazed by all the hullabaloo of the red carpet experience – although I would have loved to have had Reese as my date. She'd recently been voted again as one of the 100 Sexiest Women in the World, but I could have told them that (and who, in dog's name, were the other ninety-nine?).

For me, being on the red carpet was just another chance to be kissed and petted, held and cuddled. Everyone praised me and told me how much they loved me, so what was not to like? I always received extra treats for acting and didn't mind the noise and the fuss at all, even when the paparazzi screamed my name so loud it hurt my little terrier ears.

The only downside was all the cameras flashing in my face. I never shied away from them, like some stars do, but I didn't like that annoying white spot that remained in front of my eyes for ages afterwards, not least because it blocked my view of Dad and his all-important pockets.

To our surprise and delight, *The Artist* won three Globes, as chosen by the Hollywood Foreign Press Association. It was awarded prizes for Best Motion Picture (Comedy or Musical), Best Actor for Jean, and Best Original Score for composer Ludovic Bource (I still couldn't get that catchy theme tune out of my furry ears).

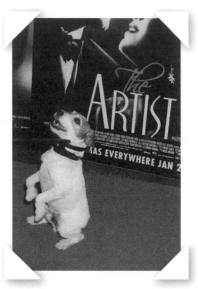

Thinking about leaving a p-mail on the red carpet.

By now an old hand at accepting awards, I bounced up onto the stage with the rest of the cast to thank presenter Jane Fonda (was it me, or does she remind anyone else of a Norwich terrier?).

Omar, keen to remain behind the scenes, handed my leash over to Jean, who was clearly delighted to see me. As the charming producer Thomas Langmann began his acceptance speech with an emotional tribute to his late father, Jean began to try out his old cues on me. Delighted to be back in his playful company, I did as he asked – walking across the stage on my back legs and playing dead when he pretended to shoot me. It was only when we heard the audience laugh and break into applause that we remembered where we were, and we realised that poor Thomas had been forced to stop speaking because of our antics.

Oops, or, as the French would say, *oups!*

There was better still to come. During the post-show photo-shoot, we were led into a room with at least a hundred reporters and photographers waiting, all shouting and shooting at the same time.

'Are you sure the dog will be able to handle all that noise and the flashes?' someone asked Dad, just before we went in. They were clearly concerned for me.

'He'll be fine,' Omar reassured them. We walked in to what I can only describe as a barrage of light and sound, and I just took it all in my doggy stride. So much so that when the Golden Globe was placed on the floor next to me in front of the cast line-up, I sidled up to it and put my paw on top of it as if it were mine.

Omar hadn't prompted me to do it, and there'd been no cues. It was just there, and I thought it seemed like the right thing to do. He was blown away, and everyone else was, too. There was a great shot taken with them all laughing at what I did.

In the next room, a full press conference was set up and waiting for the human cast to sit down and answer questions. Not believing that we would be needed, I waited just outside with Omar, but no sooner had the press conference begun than the reporters started to call, 'Where's the dog? Where's Uggie?' The

Scene stealing again at
the Golden Globes.

cast rolled their eyes a little, and Omar had no choice but to bring me in.

As one of my co-stars, Missi Pyle, said later, 'They say you're not supposed to work with children and dogs ... This dog is ridiculous ... We were doing some press, and he is a total scene stealer.'

## 31

I ACT INSTINCTIVELY. THAT'S WHY I
CAN'T PLAY ANY ROLE THAT ISN'T BASED
ON SOMETHING IN MY LIFE.
*Ethel Waters*

The world went crazy for me, it seemed, and my diary had never been fuller. I did press every day, taped an interview with Ryan Seacrest for a pre-Oscars feature, and made features in *W*, *Time*, and *Newsweek* magazines, as well as scores of publications around the globe.

Then I went on *The Ellen DeGeneres Show* to strut my stuff. Bless her, she is such a dog lover that the moment she saw me shaking, she asked Dad if I was all right. He quickly reassured her that I wasn't nervous or cold, just a bit trembly. Then, as she stood centre stage with him, I skated in, stage right, on my board, turned on it in motion, and then skated along up on my back legs.

Ellen, who was funny for a human, commented, 'My dog won't even walk on hardwood floors!'

Then Omar suggested to Ellen, 'Why don't you try it?'

'Skateboarding?' she asked, which raised another laugh.

He gave her some cubes of vegan cheese (Ellen is vegan, and he didn't want to offend her with meat). She pretended to eat them before he showed her how to encourage me to speak with the shake of a cheese-filled hand.

I then walked towards her as she stepped backwards (using the all-important sign language of two fingers beckoning upwards), and then she shot me with the word 'Bang!' and I dutifully rolled over and played dead.

Showing Ellen DeGeneres how to cross a floor, Uggie style.

When she kissed me on the nose, I did 'Shy' and hid my head for so long that she had to feed me my treat under my armpit. I received a standing ovation as Ellen announced, 'That's hilarious! He's the greatest dog!'

I couldn't disagree.

A few days later, I shot a special black-and-white feature for CBS's *Entertainment Tonight* with a pretty young actress who was sweet, but could never steal my heart from Reese. The idea was that I was supposed to be her Oscars date. Dressed in a bow tie, I met her in a fancy restaurant, where she was served caviar. 'It stinks!' I barked (as the words came up on the screen).

In its place, I was served a huge bone.

Now, that was more like it.

A few days later, I was in New York, and we were invited onto the popular morning TV show *The View* with Penelope Ann Miller. There, I sat on the bench seat and then performed a couple of stunts for the presenters. Backstage, Barbara Walters asked Omar if she could adopt me (the answer was no), and on stage, I kissed Whoopi Goldberg so much that she announced afterwards, 'That was the best action I've had in years!'

Later that day, I was skateboarding 86 stories up on the observatory deck of the Empire State Building, and in a chilly wind. We were surrounded by the world's press calling, 'Work it!' or 'Over the shoulder, Uggie.' I'm not saying that I was suffering a bit from all the different time zones I was crossing, but I have to admit to falling asleep in Omar's arms during questions.

I'd tried not to let Dad see, but I was beginning to slow down a little. For a dog, time dashes at a breakneck speed, and I'd aged nine years in canine terms since we'd shot the movie. Although I was still very active and only slightly past my prime, in my opinion I was no longer a puppy, and Omar often outpaced me.

Smooching with Whoopi Goldberg
on *The View*.

In the middle of all the press interviews we were doing for *The Artist*, I was booked for a Valentine's Day skateboarding shoot for a commercial. Apparently, I looked up at Omar with an expression that he read as, 'I'm too tired to do this, Dad.'

Nodding his understanding, he led me off set and switched Dash in for me. So it was my younger 'brother', not me, who dressed up as a gondolier and rowed down a mock-Venetian canal singing 'That's *Amore!*'

Personally, I don't recall that moment (maybe I was asleep), but Omar still got emotional talking about it a year later. 'That's when it really hit me,' he said, welling up. 'I realised Uggie wasn't going to be around forever, and I wanted him to enjoy what time he had left.'

Sure, I was pooped. Who wouldn't be, with our schedule? Even so, I was surprised when Dad made a public announcement that I'd be taking some more time out to rest, once all the hoopla over *The Artist* was over. He also declared that I wouldn't take on such a demanding role in the future.

My co-star Bérénice Bejo commented, 'Uggie heard that Brad Pitt was going to stop working for a year, and he is smart, so he told us that he was going to do the same.'

Well, if it's good enough for Mr Pitt …

What I hadn't expected (or especially wanted) was the intrusive media speculation about the decision to let me rest. I guess that kind of thing goes with the territory. Some of the newspaper headlines were unnecessarily blunt: 'Uggie Retiring Early Due to Mystery Illness' or 'Uggie to Hang Up His Collar', they declared.

As if I could ever truly step away from the spotlight – with this face!

The articles that accompanied the headlines were equally sensational:

You would never have guessed the canine star was bravely struggling with a neurological disorder throughout filming of the near-silent Oscar favourite. Now it's been revealed that the ten-year-old Jack Russell, who will retire from feature film-making after the Academy Awards ceremony, is leaving the biz due to a mystery illness that has baffled experts and cost his trainer thousands of dollars in vets' bills.

I pay my own way, thank you very much.

Omar was quoted as saying, 'It comes and goes and, ironically, it is worse when he's relaxed. When we were filming, you could hardly notice it. It is a shame this has happened when he is getting the biggest success of his career, but we feel it's the best thing to do.'

Well, we'll have to see about that.

Greta Garbo may have slipped away from the limelight at the peak of her career. So did Grace Kelly and Doris Day. Joaquin Phoenix threatened to quit after *Walk the Line* (with, aaah, Reese!), but I wasn't convinced.

This old dog isn't finished yet.

## I WAS BORN TO ACT AND LIFE ITSELF
## IS THE GREATEST PART.
### *Eva Gabor*

In the build-up to the Oscars, the awards kept coming in fast. I'd been nominated in the first ever Golden Collar Awards for my roles in *The Artist* and *Water for Elephants*. With a rare double listing, it looked like I was a shoo-in.

Could there be a chance Reese might present it to me, if I won? The thought quickened my heartbeat, but I hardly dared hope.

As so often happens in Hollywood, however, there was a little jealousy and resentment at how big a slice of the awards cake I was taking. Other canine nominees for the Golden Collar included Denver as 'Skeletor' in *50/50*, and Hummer as 'Dolce' in *Young Adult*.

My chief rival, however, (in what most pundits considered a two-dog race), was a Jack Russell named Arthur, who'd been picked over me for the role of 'Cosmo' in the movie *Beginners*, which ended up co-starring Christopher Plummer and Ewan McGregor.

I had nothing against Arthur. In fact, I'd never met the pup, and he looked like a nice enough guy (although I personally thought him a tad scruffy for our kind of work). What I was disappointed to discover was that he was considerably abetted in his talents as an actor, by the fact that his 'thoughts' appeared as subtitles on the screen.

I didn't even have those, and I was in a silent movie, for dog's sake!

Then I learned that he was really all white and not a broken coat like me. He'd had his brown bits painted on for the part. I supposed it would help him hide from the paparazzi when he was off duty, but I wasn't sure that Arthur was strictly playing by the rules.

To add insult to injury, his co-star Christopher Plummer unexpectedly announced, 'Between Cosmo and Uggie, I think our Cosmo was more human … Uggie was just a trickster … Our dog had soul.' He added later, '[Cosmo] was much more human, and actually much more professional, than Uggie. Uggie was such a circus dog. You never got to know him inside. The true Uggie never came out.'

I'd been warned by Omar that as soon as anyone made it to the top in Hollywood, there were plenty of people who would try to tear them down, but that really made my fur curl.

In true silent screen idol style, however, I refused to respond.

Just when I thought things couldn't get worse, the respected director Martin Scorsese got involved, decreeing that Blackie, the (she-dog) Doberman who'd played 'Maximillian' in his movie *Hugo*, deserved a nomination for the Golden Collar Awards as well. Scorsese went on *Ellen* and wrote an open letter to the *LA Times*, insisting that Blackie gave 'an uncompromising performance as a ferocious guard dog who terrorises children'.

He went on: 'While I have been extremely heartened by the reception of my movie *Hugo*, I feel that there is one area where we've been severely slighted. Imagine my surprise when I heard the nominations for the first Golden Collar Awards for Best Dog in a Theatrical Film ... I listened in vain for Blackie's name to be called, and then to all the hullabaloo over a certain Jack Russell terrier named Uggie.'

Although he admitted that I gave a wonderful performance and was 'a great dog', he went on to deride me as 'a nice little mascot who does tricks'. He blamed anti-Doberman prejudice for the omission. 'I detect another, more deep-seated prejudice at work. Jack Russell terriers were bred in the nineteenth century for the purposes of fox-hunting by an Englishman, the Rev. John Russell. Dobermans were bred by a German tax collector who was afraid of being bludgeoned to death by the citizenry. But does that mean we must condemn the entire breed?'

Under such high-profile pressure, the event's organisers, Dog News Daily, announced that if 500 members of the public 'liked' Blackie's Facebook page, she'd be nominated. They did, and she was. 'Due to the outpouring of love and support from around the world from fans of Mr Scorsese, his film *Hugo*, and its canine star Blackie, the write-in campaign … for Blackie has been successful,' announced a spokesman.

Well, bring it on then.

Dog News Daily nominations for
Best Dog in a Theatrical Film.

On the night of the Golden Collar Awards at the Hyatt Regency Century Plaza hotel (which was streamed to 150 million people in more than 25 countries around the globe), I put my best paw forward and took sunglasses in case the flashbulbs threatened my retinas again. I was nervous but quietly confident at the table I shared with Omar and my co-stars from *The Artist*, Missi Pyle, James Cromwell, and Beth Grant.

James, who played the chauffeur in *The Artist* (and at 6 feet 7 inches is the tallest human I have ever met), was a true gentleman who became a good buddy to Omar and me. He was an ardent campaigner for animal rights – especially pigs – and had been nominated for an Academy Award for Best Supporting Actor for his role in the movie *Babe*, which featured a pig.

Now, I like pigs – they are really smart – but the concern among a lot of canine thespians is that they could snaffle work from under our noses if we let them, so the less said about *Babe* the better. In spite of his hog-loving tendencies, however, James was kind enough to tell anyone who would listen that 'Uggie is wonderfully trained and talented. I'd like to see a special Oscar recognising the achievements of animals.'

When the announcement came at the Golden Collar Awards that I'd won the title Best Dog in a Theatrical Film, I was a little starstruck. Actress Wendie Malick (who repeatedly pronounced my name 'You-gie' for some reason), presented the award to Omar, who carried me up to the podium. He showed me the gold and Swarovski-crystal-encrusted collar set on a paw-shaped Plexiglas holder, but I was too overcome to bark.

Accompanied on the stage by my sister Terry and the lovely Sarah Clifford, Omar spoke for me when he said that being picked for the award was 'overwhelming'.

He told Dog News Daily, 'This is very important for all the trainers in the movie industry, because we have never been recognised before, and people just don't understand that it takes hundreds and even thousands of hours to train a dog.'

There was never a truer word spoken.

He then brought a tear to my eye when he kissed me and added: 'The one person that I would really like to thank – who is very, very special – is Uggie. He has been my buddy forever and is a great performer and great family member. He sleeps with us and he's getting kind of old ...'

Hey! Speak for yourself, Pops.

Omar congratulating me at the
Golden Collar Awards.

## ACTING ISN'T REALLY A
## CREATIVE PROFESSION. IT'S AN
## INTERPRETIVE ONE.
### *Paul Newman*

It was hard not to get too used to all these accolades, when a week later I also won the 'Pawscar' for Best Scene Stealer from the American Humane Association.

Pronounced 'Poskers', they are awarded each year in recognition of the year's best animal performances. The AHA advocates the proper treatment of animals on the thousands of movies that are granted its 'no animals were harmed' certification.

A spokesman for the AHA said, 'Uggie can evoke more humour and light-heartedness in silence and in black and white than most dogs can in Technicolor and sound. Not only did Uggie steal the hearts of *The Artist*'s audience, he also stole the hearts of his co-stars.'

Tell that to those sausage-coveting extras!

*The Artist* continued to shine, as well, winning Best Film at the Césars in Paris and at the Indie Spirit Awards in Santa Monica. It had 10 nominations pending at the Academy Awards, which was set for the end of February.

As if a Pawscar wasn't enough, I was asked to co-present the 26th annual Genesis Awards at the Beverly Hilton Hotel, attended by a host of stars – canine, feline, avian, and human. As part of a long-standing campaign by the Humane Society of the United States, the awards recognised the entertainment industry for raising awareness of animal protection. So, off we went again in another limo for another night celebrating Hollywood animals.

Another day, another limo.
With Mercy and Omar.

My fellow host was Carrie Ann Inaba from *Dancing with the Stars*, and I was delighted when *The Ellen DeGeneres Show* and Animal Planet were both honoured for their work. In my back-stage dressing room, I was presented with a huge gift basket full of collars, leashes, treats, and toys – my first ever goody bag! More were to follow.

Humbled as I was by all the plaudits, I have to confess to being even more excited to learn that a New York bakery named Eleni's, which made Oscar-season confections, had created a cookie that looked like me. Sadly, I never got to taste one. My bitterness was sweetened by the news that although Scorsese's *Hugo* was also represented in Eleni's Oscar-themed offerings, it was symbolised not by Blackie the Doberman, but by a clock.

Sorry, Marty!

The telephone never stopped ringing with requests for media interviews, or for my appearance at some event or other. I also received an invitation from *The Washington Times*, that was addressed to me 'and my human companion', to attend the White House Correspondents' Dinner in Washington DC on 28 April 2012, as an honoured guest. The annual black-tie gala for journalists, politicians, and celebrities, and attended by the President and First Lady, had previously welcomed Frank Sinatra, Ray Charles, Bob Hope, and Aretha Franklin.

I'd give it a go, but I hoped they knew that my singing voice was more of a howl.

A host of Hollywood stars had also been invited, including George Clooney (we could compare dentistry), Goldie Hawn (a tail-wagging golden retriever of a human), and Piers Morgan, a British terrier of an interviewer. I also hoped to meet Bo, the presidential Portuguese water spaniel, and his humans, Mr and Mrs O.

The most exciting news of all, though, was that Reese Witherspoon had been asked to the event as a guest of *Newsweek* magazine. I was so enraptured at the thought that my body went into a fresh spasm of limb shivering, which almost made Omar take me back to the vet. I had to control myself just to reassure him. Trembling inside, I was beside myself with excitement and hardly dared hope that I might get to see my beloved again.

In the inimitable words of Monsieur H.'s adored Cole Porter: 'Day and night, night and day, under the hide of me, there's an oh such a hungry yearning burning inside of me ...'

Oh Reese, how I've missed you!

## MARTYRDOM WAS THE PRICE OF
## ENTHUSIASM FOR ACTING.
### *Bela Lugosi*

As the 'O' night loomed, so my roll call of public appearances seemed endless. My mail bag was groaning with fan letters and gifts such as collars and treats (Omar kept strict control of those). I also received more fancy embossed invitations addressed to: 'Uggie plus one'.

Fat Popeye was beside himself with jealousy, although he had no reason to be, because he skateboarded beautifully with Julio and Gordo on a commercial for Smart Water co-starring Jennifer Aniston, who is pretty hot, to my mind.

A few weeks before the 'big night', I was invited onto *Jimmy Kimmel Live!* – a popular late-night talk show on ABC. Jimmy had an annual tradition of inviting remarkable animals onto his show to 'prognosticate' the winners of the Academy Awards. In 2011 it was Heidi, the cross-eyed possum, but sadly, she had since died.

In her place, I was asked to burst through a crimson curtain, trot down a red carpet, and stand on a podium every night for a week before choosing from a line-up of celebrity photographs (each one adorned with an identical hot-dog treat).

For Best Actress I picked Meryl Streep – after wavering around Viola Davis, as so many of us voters did. For Best Actor, I went for George Clooney – sorry, Jean, but George was outstanding in *The Descendants*, and he did have to learn a lot of lines. I redeemed myself slightly by selecting the hot dog balanced on the top of the poster for *The Artist* as Best Picture (although I also grabbed the snack on top of *Hugo* by way of an oblique apology to Blackie).

I had a lot of fun, treats, and kisses on the show, and then Omar took me home. Much to our dismay, though, my appearance on national television created an unforeseen scandal of epic proportions. A sharp-eyed, but ill-informed, member of the show's staff spotted that my markings were different from those I'd had painted onto my neck in *The Artist* (to look like my understudy Dash, if you recall).

'The patch does not match!' Jimmy Kimmel declared with mock outrage soon afterwards. Instead of checking the facts with Omar, he went on to suggest to the nation that I might have been an imposter who'd tricked him, Ellen, and the good people at the Golden Globes by swapping places with 'the real Uggie'.

To compound his insult, he dubbed me 'the fake Uggie' – or 'Fuggie'.

He added, 'I'm wondering now if Ugg boots are really even made of dog fur!' He claimed to have summoned the FBI to investigate, but they weren't interested, so he threatened to bring in Dog the Bounty Hunter instead.

Dash thought the whole thing was hilarious, and I had to curl my lip at him on more than one occasion. I also flashed a polished incisor at that grimacing cur Popeye. Omar was as cross as I was and spent a lot of time on the telephone to the people at the Kimmel show, demanding a chance to explain.

Quite aside from the public humiliation, I was worried that the identity scandal might affect my security clearance for the White House dinner.

After some debate, Omar and I were finally invited back onto the show via a video link, so that we could set the record straight.

'There is no Fuggie,' Omar told Mr Kimmel, wagging a finger at him (which I knew meant bad boy). 'There is only one Uggie, right here.'

I sat next to him on the couch, alert and ears cocked, making sure that he argued my case well. 'There was no switching,' Omar insisted. 'Uggie was the main character in the movie. And just like people, he had to have make-up. We had three dogs, and they all had to match each other. All the white around his eyes was covered, and we used a lot of colour, not just on his head, but all over his body, to make a lot of different patches.'

(Okay, okay, I take it all back, Cosmo.)

Omar reiterated that I'd only been made up with exactly the same markings as Dash, in case he had to step in as an understudy. It was never needed, but I had to keep that make-up on throughout the film, just in case. Mr K. retorted that Omar sounded suspicious, because he has an accent and is foreign.

My response to his insult was to bow my head in my bashful routine, but he interpreted that as 'shame'. If he'd been there in the room with me, I'd have given his nostrils something to be really ashamed of.

Dash and Dude attempting to
emulate my movie-star looks.

To prove his point, Omar summoned Dash and Dude up onto the sofa to show how similar we looked. He explained how Dude and I had to be made up to match Dash's longer brown patch – or, as I like to call it, blemish.

'There is only one Uggie,' Omar declared. 'The others were just there in case Uggie got sick or injured, but Uggie was the one who did all the work.'

Tell me about it. Even as a seasoned actor, that movie took a lot out of me.

'Dude is kinda fat!' Kimmel suddenly announced, cleverly directing the attention away from his blunder. 'Why does he weigh 40 pounds more than the others?'

'He's been eating,' Omar admitted with a slightly guilty smile. 'He's been off for the past three years, just relaxing in the house, so that's what happens.'

'Let that be a warning to all dogs,' responded the host.

For the first time, I felt sorry for poor Dude, even though he'd inadvertently defused the tension of Fuggie-Gate once and for all.

## 35

### IF YOUR DOG DOESN'T LIKE SOMEONE,
### YOU PROBABLY SHOULDN'T EITHER.
### *Unknown*

One of the consequences of all this attention and publicity was that there was a worldwide spike in the demand for Jack Russell terriers. It became known as the 'Uggie effect'.

My success had apparently unleashed a new craze, with hundreds of would-be owners contacting shelters and dog homes across America and Europe. Even the future king of England, Prince Charles, loves Jack Russells and had recently picked up a third from a rescue centre.

Scram, corgis!

At Battersea Dogs and Cats Home in London, England, almost a thousand people searched on its website for a dog that looked like me after they'd watched the BAFTAs. This was more than double the number on the previous week and the highest number of enquiries for any other night of the year. There were similar tales elsewhere.

Dogs of my breed – which comprised 8 per cent of all the home's strays – became the second most popular to be rehomed after Staffordshire bull terriers (are you kidding me?). That was a leap of three places on the 'Wanted' list. Battersea's rehoming coordinator Carly Perry said, 'Jack Russells are always a popular breed, but this current increase in demand is giving them the opportunity to really enjoy their fame. Although we're pleased, we want to make sure people who do find their own Uggie are aware of the level of commitment required to own a pet.'

Owners were warned that taking any animal involved daily and lifelong care. They encouraged proper research to ensure that the right environment was provided. The Jack Russell Terrier Club of America warned that even experienced dog owners can be overwhelmed by the demands of a Jack.

'Russells are first and foremost hunting dogs,' a spokeswoman pointed out. 'The traits and skills that make them excellent hunting dogs – digging, barking, an aggressive nature, and an ability to follow scent – are often interpreted as bad habits that cause people to give them up.' She worried that the breed was only 'hot' thanks to *The Artist*, and that when the fad wore off (me, wear off?), rescue homes might have to pick up the pieces and find new homes for rejected Jacks.

The news was alarming, and I didn't want any unwanted pooches on my conscience. Omar and I had long been committed to supporting rescue homes and shelters in any way we could, and we wanted to do more. If I was a rich celebrity, I'd have donated a lot of money to them, but sadly there were no residuals for the likes of me, so we came up with another idea: auctioning off headshots of my face on eBay, complete with an inky paw print, or pawtograph. Omar added the words 'Best Wishes, Omar von Muller and Uggie' and sold them to raise much-needed funds for a number of his favourite rescue charities. I also offered my services to PETA (People for the Ethical

My charity pawtograph
for rescue dogs.

Treatment of Animals) with a poster of me featuring the words: 'I'm Uggie, and I was adopted. Millions of dogs are waiting in animal shelters for a loving home. Adopt, Don't Buy.'

As I told my fans on my social networking sites, 'If we all get our dog poop together, we can help thousands of needy dogs out there. Lots of licks, Uggie xx.'

And that's what we have continued to do.

**36**

STARDOM IS ONLY A BY-PRODUCT
OF ACTING. I DON'T THINK BEING A
MOVIE STAR IS A GOOD ENOUGH
REASON FOR EXISTING.
*Natalie Wood*

The night we were meeting Oscar was 26 February 2012, and I was determined to take it all in my stride, even though I'd just celebrated my 10th birthday, which made me 70 in human years.

The humans were definitely more excited than usual. The names of those of us involved with *The Artist* had been trending on Facebook and Twitter for weeks, and everyone had been getting ready for hours. With Mom and Dad looking good and smelling sweet, we were ready to go. Popeye's farewell gas was unwelcome, but not entirely unexpected, and even he couldn't hide his excitement. (I'd appeased him by telling him that he and Gordo could be my bodyguards, in case of any dognapping attempts.)

We were driven to Hollywood in a big, black limousine, and Dad let me hang out of the window with my tongue out just to catch the breeze. Always a joy.

I reflected back on my day, during which I'd been treated to a pampering day courtesy of the press at the fabled Chateau Marmont Hotel on Sunset Boulevard. In a beautiful suite, I was given a shampoo and blow-dry by a grooming consultant. Then I wandered around the gardens and relieved myself where some of the Hollywood greats such as Douglas Fairbanks Jr and Greta Garbo had once stood sipping Martinis.

That was quite a moment.

First stop was the Soho House Hotel, where we'd been invited to a pre-Oscars soirée. The paparazzi went crazy for me, calling out, 'Uggie, over here!' or 'Uggie, this way!'

Baby, I worked that carpet.

Inside, the place was packed wall-to-wall with celebs, and I was passed from one to the other like a lucky charm. Everyone wanted to touch me, hold me, kiss me, stroke me, and have their photos taken with me.

You do what you have to do.

Notable groupies (or 'Uggie Huggers' as I like to call them) included the blue-coat Katy Perry, who posted a picture of me in her arms on Twitter with the line: 'Catch of the Day! Uggie from *The Artist*.'

All I can say in response is, 'She kissed a dog, and she liked it …'

The actor Gerard Butler, whom I'd first met on *The Graham Norton Show* in London, spotted me across the room and came running over to scoop me into his arms with a cry of 'Uggie! You have no idea how starstruck I am!'

I kept my eyes peeled for Reese, but she was nowhere to be seen, sadly. Was she avoiding me? Had she gone looking for me at another party? Were the rumours that she'd remarried true? Or was she keeping away, so as not to steal my limelight?

Remembering my unfortunate experience with champagne, I stuck to water, to keep my wits about me – and help wash down all those icky designer cosmetics I was constantly expected to lick. I also gratefully accepted every canapé that was offered to me (how come I'd never tried smoked salmon before? Yummy!).

Jean Dujardin was there and kept grabbing me for another French kiss, which the photographers were happy to record, as he told everyone how much he loved me. I suspect he had not stuck to water.

'There was no competition between us,' he insisted, when a reporter asked about working with me. 'Uggie was my shadow and my friend. I wasn't a dog lover before I met him, but now I am … It was actually quite easy to work with him, because he's a really well-trained dog. Very talented.'

*J'adore Jean.*

Monsieur H. was a little less complimentary, but I put it down to nerves.

'I'm afraid Uggie could become a little bit megalomaniac if he won an Oscar,' he said. 'You know how actors are … When

I worked with him, he was satisfied to work with other dog characters, so I am afraid that maybe he's going to think that he is such a great actor that he is going to want to play some other characters, not just dogs – maybe cats or horses. I hope he will stay humble.'

Me? Play a cat?

Purr-leeze!

Harvey Weinstein dubbed me his 'secret weapon' and added magnanimously, 'Uggie's right up there with the big ones.'

All too soon, it was time to leave for the ceremony. As we approached the famous former Kodak Theatre, we could hear the fans going crazy, so I drew my head in from the open window and hid behind the limo's tinted glass, in case I was mobbed. There was such a crush of people and press that I didn't even get the chance to inspect the stars on the Hollywood Walk of Fame (or relieve myself once more on Lassie's).

To my disappointment, we were quickly driven around backstage, instead of joining the long line of celebrities heading inside the 3,000-seat theatre. What was going on?

I was 'The Ugg-ster' and I was ready for my close-up, Mr DeMille.

'Who are you wearing tonight, Uggie?' I'd expected Joan Rivers to shout at me from behind banks of dazzling TV lights.

At which point, I planned to turn to the camera and pose in my 18-carat-gold neckpiece with a look that said, 'Nothing but a bow tie and a smile, darling!'

Then I remembered – it was meant to be a huge secret that I was attending at all!

**Posing for some of my fans in Hollywoodland.**

There'd been all sorts of speculation that I hadn't been invited to the Oscars ceremony, and people had been widely indignant on my behalf. What they didn't know was that I had always been invited, but that it was meant to be a big surprise. The show's veteran host, Billy Crystal, had even been working behind the scenes with me for an opening skit.

In fact, Billy and I had shot an entire pre-Oscars spread for *Entertainment Weekly*, which was planned to feature him and me on the cover. The last time a Jack Russell had a cover feature in that magazine it was Moose ('Eddie') from *Frasier* in the 1990s, so I was thrilled to be following in such illustrious pawsteps. Annoyingly, some naysayer said that, as I was in *The Artist*, that would be showing favouritism, so the spread was pulled.

Billy and I still had our skit to do, though, so just before the lights went up at the Oscars, I was led in the dark to a seat in the front row, waiting for my big 'reveal'. Sitting there in silence, my nostrils were overwhelmed by perfume and cologne.

The music started, the opening film rolled, and everyone started to relax as Billy sped through his take on the year's best movie moments and then burst through onto the stage. A few moments later, he was cracking jokes. 'This is a pressure-packed night for a lot of you, and the nominees are sitting in the audience and people are wondering, "What are they thinking?"' He claimed to have a psychic gift and said that when the camera focused on a celebrity, he'd be able to tell what their thoughts were.

First up was Brad Pitt, and Billy claimed he was thinking, 'This better not go too late, I have six parent-teacher conferences in the morning.'

Next was Morgan Freeman and Billy impersonated him narrating *The March of the Penguins* (a great movie for a sticky California day, by the way).

George Clooney's thoughts were supposed to be: 'Billy, you didn't tell me that kiss was being filmed!' Viola Davis was supposed to be thanking her agent for a role of a strong black woman not played by Tyler Perry (a man). Martin Scorsese was allegedly giving directions: 'Ready Camera Two, take Marty ... push in ... no, push back, he looks too serious.' For Nick Nolte, Billy just grunted incomprehensively.

Then my face came up on screen – the only one to get a ripple of applause and an 'Aaaah' from the crowd. As I gave a joyful bark on cue, Billy spoke the words he said were in my head.

'If I had them I'd lick 'em! If I had them I'd lick 'em!'

Spookily, that wasn't too far from the truth.

Then the award-giving began and, boy, what a night it turned out to be. After the success of the Best Actor award at Cannes, three Golden Globes, seven BAFTAs and six Césars (becoming the most awarded film in French history), *The Artist* won five of its 10 Oscar nominations, including Best Picture, Best Director, and Best Actor.

That's the human equivalent of three Golden Collars.

Awesome, guys!

When Jean came off stage having just collected his golden statuette, he grabbed hold of me, pressed me to him and, full of emotion, cried, 'Thank you, buddy! Thank you so much!'

I, too, was overcome. Someone took a photo of me licking the full length of Jean's face with a grateful pink tongue.

At the end of the show, when *The Artist* won the Oscar for Best Picture, Omar proudly led me up onto the stage with the rest of the cast. Only this time, Jean and I knew better than to fool around.

When Monsieur H. went up to collect his prize, he listed all those he had to thank, including the producer, cast, and crew. He finally conceded, 'I want to thank Uggie the dog …' (which I was pleased to hear got another ripple of applause and an affectionate laugh).

Congratulating my co-star
Jean Dujardin at the Oscars.

Then he added, 'I think he doesn't care …'
(Me, not care?)
'I'm not sure he understands what I say …'
(With that accent? True, Monsieur.)
'He's not that good …'
What??
In spite of his aside, I am so terribly proud of what happened that night. Everyone thought Monsieur H. was barking mad to make a black-and-white silent movie, but he proved them all

wrong. His charming Valentine to Hollywood's golden age cost $15 million to make but had already earned almost $100 million worldwide. Somebody wise at the *New York Times* said it should be called 'The Artists' because of the invaluable contribution each of us made to its success, and he spoke the truth.

If Omar was right and I never made another movie, I didn't mind so much. The saying goes that you are only as good as your last movie. Having a career-defining role in *The Artist* had been a once-in-a-lifetime experience – especially for a dog – and one that was unlikely ever to be matched.

I had achieved that rarest of gifts: Hollywood immortality.

Should that be the end of my moments on the silver screen, then maybe it was time to 'send the elevator back down', as Jack Lemmon once said. There were plenty of up-and-coming pups ready to step onto my mark, including young Dash.

I couldn't think of a better way to take my final bow.

## THE MORE PEOPLE I MEET,
## THE MORE I LIKE MY DOG.
### *Unknown*

The aftershow parties at the Oscars are legendary and, suffice it to say, 2012 was no exception. At the Weinstein Company's glitzy affair at the Mondrian Hotel on Sunset Boulevard, I was hugged and kissed and squeezed so much that Omar had to take me to a side booth for a little peace.

It was already late and we had a 5 a.m. start the next day in order to appear on the national TV breakfast show *Live! with Kelly*. I didn't want the night to end, but I was exhausted, and even the heady scent of cocktail sausages couldn't keep me going.

In the end, I could hardly keep my eyes open, and a few of the paparazzi caught me yawning. Omar eventually persuaded me to kiss everyone goodbye and give up my quest for Reese.

'We still have a lot of work to do, buddy,' he reminded me.

He was right, of course. My post-ceremony schedule would have rivalled that of any Oscar nominee, and I was more popular than many of my two-legged co-stars. With my itinerary booked solid with events and appearances, I really needed some beauty sleep.

Driving home in the limo in the early hours, I stuck my head out of the window as I stared at the passing lights of Tinseltown. Pointing my nose at the Dog Stars I howled my thanks for being given my chance to shine.

One of my first appearances after the show was to attend the annual Oscar round-table discussion for *Newsweek*, hosted by George Clooney. When they arrived for the photoshoot, Tilda Swinton and Charlize Theron actually fought over me, and Charlize squeezed me so tight I went a little dizzy. Tilda eventually won the tussle by folding herself in two to kneel in front of my face and let me lick all the make-up off her. Their ardent attention made me feel a little less uncomfortable, because Christopher Plummer was also there, although the grumpy old grey-coat mercifully ignored me.

When George arrived at the studio for filming and the photoshoot, he spotted me and asked Omar, 'Is that Uggie?' and then cried, 'Okay! That's it. We're walking out!' before flashing me that megawatt smile of his. A devoted animal lover, he readily agreed to have his picture taken with me and the rest of the round-table crew.

Next up was my presence at various events to celebrate the announcement that I'd been chosen to be the spokesdog for the DS computer game Nintendogs+cats.

This was my first big sponsorship deal! Are you listening out there, sausage makers of the world?

What Omar and I liked most about the game was that it taught children how to become more responsible pet owners. They chose a puppy and then they had to feed it, take it for walks, and play with it. The technology was incredible. The dog recognised its 'owner's' voice, and players could teach their dogs obedience with a few routines. They could even compete with them at dog shows featuring other players' dogs. Amazing.

My sister Terry loved playing the game but, to be honest, I'd rather she played with the real thing – a.k.a. award-winning *moi!* I watched the screen and listened to the little computer puppy barking and wondered what all the fuss was about.

I mean, why nibble kibble when you've got pizza on your plate?

Nintendo shot a special video, which shows me arriving in a tie for my first day at their offices. I have to put my paw print on some publicity photographs and am served my lunch in a bowl at my new desk. Then 'the boss' arrives, and I look up fearfully, only to see Super Mario waving and smiling at me. The final frame is me giving him a wink.

Making the video was a lot of fun and not nearly as intense as making a movie, for which my quivering bones were grateful. And the company seemed delighted to have me. 'Uggie didn't have to sit up and beg for his role as Nintendo's spokesdog,' Scott Moffitt, the brand's executive vice-president of sales and marketing, said later. 'It's truly our pleasure to work with a star of Uggie's magnitude.'

Now, that's more like it!

Not long afterwards, we were asked to go to the Hollywood Boulevard Mall to shoot a sequence for Japanese TV. Generally speaking, I was able to get away without being recognised. Jack Russells are common, and my true markings are slightly different to those in the movie.

Once Omar and I started getting such intense media coverage together, however, we were recognised more and more. As soon as the cameras began to roll and I began showing off some of my thespian skills at the mall, people started crowding in to take their own photographs. Before we knew it, people were screaming my name and we were completely swamped.

'It was scary,' Omar told Mercy later. 'Uggie's such a little guy, and I was worried he was going to get trampled underfoot. I had to scoop him up and pretty much run out of there, just to get him to safety.'

From that day on, he was much more wary of taking me to crowded places. Even walking me out in the local park late at night, he'd take Popeye or Gordo along, for extra security.

'It's crazy, but I worry that someone might try to dognap Uggie, or he might get injured in another crush of people,' Omar said. 'It's my job to protect him, and I've done a pretty good job for the last 10 years. I'm not going to let anything happen to my buddy now.'

When I was invited to be one of the stars of the 'Salute to Hollywood Pets' at the 23rd American Family Pet Expo in Orange County, California, in April 2012, Omar was equally cautious. I was assigned my own uniformed security guard, who instructed my fans to form an orderly line. It seemed that an extraordinarily high proportion of the 50,000 people who attended over three days wanted to be photographed with me.

Protected from my over-adoring
fans by Gordo and Popeye.

The more famous I became, it seemed, the less I had to do to please people. A lot of the time, I just sat around in my fake-fur bed and looked adorable, yet men, women, and children were thrilled even to see me.

'Oh, he's so cute!' they'd cry, or 'It's Uggie!' One woman was reduced to tears and several carried magazine clippings or photographs of me, which they asked Omar to sign.

What my security guard didn't protect me from, however, was a lady who turned up with a small cat in her arms and – quite literally – pushed it into my face! I could feel a stirring of old instincts within me, but Omar was pleased with how well I managed to control them. I wasn't quite so laid-back about the goat that was casually led past by an exhibitor, however. Jumping off my podium, the primordial beast in me roared. I'd have run after it and bitten its haunch in a doggy heartbeat, if Omar hadn't grabbed me by the leash.

Goat-Gate had not been forgotten.

My co-star on the stand was a fellow rescue dog named Suzie Q, a quirky-looking Chihuahua-Brussels griffon mix who played 'Jim' on *Mike & Molly*, a TV show on CBS. A few stands down sat Brigitte, who played 'Stella' in *Modern Family*, and just behind me were the dogs from the *Beverly Hills Chihuahua* movies.

Poor Suzie Q. I really felt for her having to play a character of a different gender. It may have worked for Dustin Hoffman in *Tootsie*, or Glenn Close in *Albert Nobbs*, but personally I was emotionally scarred after playing 'Queenie' in *Water for Elephants*. I must have been getting mellow in my old age, because I'd even come to feel a little sympathy for Pal playing Lassie. What a burden that must have been to bear.

Humans didn't understand what that kind of gender mix-up can do to an animal. The most I had to endure people saying was: 'Oh, he's so much smaller than he looks in the movie!'

Yeah? Well, wait until you meet Tom Cruise.

Whereas poor Suzie Q heard people cry out time and again, 'Oh, is that Jim?' or 'I love Jim! He's the best!'

I wondered what damage was being done to a dog who had never fully recovered from being sent to a pound as a puppy.

Her owner and acting coach, Sarah Cole, who'd rescued her, admitted, 'Suzie has become totally dominant over the other dogs and rules the roost completely. I think she really believes she's Jim now!'

All I could do was place a sympathetic paw on Suzie's shoulder and wish her all the best.

Giving fellow thespian Suzie Q
some moral support.

## ACTING IS LIFE TO ME,
## AND SHOULD BE.
### *Vivien Leigh*

It's not every day that you're invited to attend a gala evening with the President of the United States. Aside from the question of what to wear – the Palm Dog, or the imitation Chopard? – my biggest dilemma was what my dinner might comprise.

Had they been informed of my dietary needs? Sausages, pizza, and burgers were acceptable (hold the mustard, though). Caviar and anything feathered was out. And if I had been invited along, would Bo, the First Dog and a Portuguese water spaniel, be there, too? That would be quite a thrill.

Out of courtesy to my hosts, I'd watched a couple of Brazilian TV shows and picked up a little Portuguese in case I was to brush noses with the dog who lived in the biggest kennel in the world.

'Hello' was '*olà!*' and 'how's it going?' was '*como vai você?*' Dog was '*cao*' and sausage was '*salsicha*'. It was probably not strictly necessary, especially as Bo was born and raised in the US, but I was happy to add a little Portuguese to my repertoire of languages, now that I'd cracked English, French, and Spanish.

Uggie: The Polyglot – who knew?

There'd been an extraordinary amount of interest from the American media in the choice of Bo, which followed months of speculation as to what type of dog the President and First Lady might acquire for their daughters, who apparently suffer from allergies (few people are allergic to me).

Bo was the latest in a long line of presidential pooches, dating back to George Washington and his American stag-hounds named Sweet Lips, Scentwell, and Vulcan. Thomas Jefferson favoured briards, Andrew Jackson kept a cursing parrot instead of dogs (ugh!), Abraham Lincoln redressed that misstep with Fido and Jip, and Theodore Roosevelt went over-board with ten hounds and a zoo of other animals, including guinea pigs, a snake, and a badger.

John F. Kennedy kept seven dogs at the White House, including a poodle, a Welsh terrier, and a German shepherd. Ronald Reagan loved dogs and had six, including a Bouvier des Flandres, and Bill Clinton had Buddy, a chocolate Labrador who sparked a craze for the soppy-hearted mutts.

From what I could gather, a Jack Russell had never sported the address 1600 Pennsylvania Avenue, Washington DC on its tag.

There was still time.

I was a little galled to know that Lassie (a.k.a. a male descend-ant of Pal's) was once a guest at the White House in the 1960s.

He'd apparently been chosen as the poster dog for the 'Keep America Beautiful' campaign run by Lady Bird Johnson, the First Lady at the time. I took perverse pleasure in discovering that 'Lassie' didn't remain long at the world's most famous address after the First Dog, a white collie named Blanco, quickly ran him off the premises.

Eyeing up the presidential lawn at 1600 Pennsylvania Avenue.

Barbara Bush, the wife of George H. W. Bush, wrote a book about their dog Millie, a springer spaniel, who was once called 'the most famous dog in White House history'. President Bush said of her in a 1992 speech during his bid for re-election, 'My dog Millie knows more about foreign affairs than these two bozos,' referring to Al Gore and Bill Clinton.

Although over-sentimental – typical for a spaniel – Millie's book did give a fascinating dog's-eye view of presidential life. This included the many protocols the poor she-dog had to adhere to, such as not digging up the tulips or leaving hairs on some of the nation's most historic furniture. The best thing about it, though, to my mind, was her vivid descriptions of squirrel hunting at Camp David. That a girl!

Flying to Washington to pad the same streets as Millie and all her predecessors was quite a thrill. I had, by then, persuaded Omar that I deserved a taste of the high life, and I would only travel business class next to him. Being an Academy Award-winning star has its advantages. My wish was granted, so we hopped across the country, courtesy of American Airlines, in appropriate style.

From the moment we landed, though, my paws barely touched the ground. It had been three months since *The Artist* cleaned up at the Oscars, yet the media and public hunger for me and our movie hadn't diminished (I'm delighted to say).

Every now and again, I had to pinch myself. Could it really be that the one-time delinquent – shameless perpetrator of Cat-Gate, Goat-Gate, and Zebra-Gate – was peering up through the railings at the Oval Office, where I'm sure I could have inhaled the remnant scents of every great American leader since the days of John Adams?

Was it possible that the pooch who'd been caught red-pawed after stealing from the hand that fed him was being cooed at by adoring fans, as he left a legacy p-mail at the foot of the Lincoln Memorial? How had I ended up trotting past Capitol Hill as the (albeit temporary) King of the Hill?

We stayed at the Washington Hilton, the venue of the big event, and had lunch in the lobby restaurant on our first day. A big crowd started to gather and take photographs as we ate (is nothing private?), and then the veteran interviewer Barbara Walters (whom I'd first met backstage at *The View*) spotted me and came over to coo once again. She asked a passing guest, 'Do you know how famous Uggie is?' and he replied, 'Almost as famous as you?'

Omar told me that the hotel rules prevented me from sitting at the table with him and Mom in the grand ballroom for the dinner, but I was instead promised a 'hot date' with room service.

There'd better be sausages!

## FAME IS A FICKLE FOOD
## UPON A SHIFTING PLATE.
### *Emily Dickinson*

**A**t the pre-dinner reception, I was treated like a Hollywood superstar. With Omar squeezed into his tux and Mercy in a long white backless gown that showed off her assets, we were a little overwhelmed at first.

There were some 3,000 humans invited, and there appeared to be lots of different parties, most of which required special invitations. The minute the security guards saw me, though, we were waved straight through.

A fog of hairspray and cologne filled the air. There was a general whiff of fine scotch and vodka (and humans think it has no smell!). Waiters in white coats served champagne and canapés, and I was allowed a nibble or two.

When I wasn't eating or being cuddled, I sniffed and sniffed, but I couldn't catch a whiff of Reese anywhere.

A buzz about my arrival began to spread, and humans began to clamour around for photographs and to chat with Omar and Mercy. She, by the way, was in her element. It was as if she'd been dropped into a real-life *People* magazine, and her big brown eyes were practically popping out like those of a cartoon character.

DC Confidential with
Kevin Spacey.

One of the first people to come up and ask for a photo with me was the actor and director Kevin Spacey. He was very sweet, and as he cuddled me, Omar reminded him that they'd worked together once on a photoshoot. Mercy couldn't stop grinning.

I was much more relaxed about the whole thing and raised a friendly paw from across the room to Charlize Theron, who'd hugged me at the Oscars round-table event. I also spotted Steven Spielberg, and Eva Longoria from *Desperate Housewives* (a favourite of Jumpy's), but we didn't get a chance to talk.

The actress Rosario Dawson was all over me like a rash; she was the sweetest. There were a lot of press photographers taking pictures of us, too, and *The Washington Times* described me as 'the most sought-after celebrity' at the party. *USA Today* tweeted halfway through the reception that I was 'the sharpest dressed so far'. I was going to opt for a classic black satin bow tie, but at Mercy's suggestion I started the evening by wearing a mini tux that was a gift from the Beverly Hills Mutt Club. (The simpler bow tie was kept for more casual wear later in the evening.)

We saw the President and First Lady from afar and, bow-wow, what a beauty she was. He was smaller and thinner than he looked on the TV, but then isn't that what everyone says to me? I wanted to say hello, but they were surrounded by body-guards, and there was no sign of Bo, so sadly my Portuguese lessons were wasted.

Then came the announcement that dinner was due to be served, but I still hadn't spotted Reese. I was less than happy when Omar took me back to our room so I could slurp from a bowl of fresh water and nibble on a few of the special treats our hosts had kindly provided for me. He hid the remainder high up in a cupboard, which even I would have found impossible to open, towel or not.

He turned on the TV so I could watch the proceedings live, and then he left, locking me in the room. Dognapping was still a fear for him, but he hoped the high-profile presence of the Secret Service on every floor would keep me safe. Then he went back downstairs to take his place at a huge table, at which former Secretary of Defence Donald Rumsfeld was one of the political stars. As Mr R. told Omar how lucky he was to have Mercy, they ate shrimp risotto and steak followed by a yummy chocolate cake.

Did they save any for me? Did they heck!

Dogs seemed to feature prominently during the speeches. Apparently, in his memoir, the President had mentioned that he'd tried dog meat when he was a boy growing up in Indonesia – something his political opponents brought up to discredit him in the election campaign. The President then made a joke about eating a pit bull, which he said was delicious with a little soy sauce.

He also ran a spoof campaign video, featuring his dog Bo, about the canines of the USA leading a life of government dependency. It concluded, 'American dogs can't afford four more years of Obama (that's 28 years for them). Our dogs need leadership now.'

All this dog needed right then was a piece of juicy steak and a mouthful of shrimp risotto.

Then Jimmy Kimmel performed the traditional 'roast' of the President and said, 'Uggie is here. He is amazing. He can roll over on command. He's a Democrat.' He added, 'If the President tries to butter you, run!'

With the dinner and speeches over by 11 p.m., by which time I was rehearsing my sleep-acting, Omar and Mercy wandered around for a while. They soon realised that everyone important seemed to be slipping away to the various after-dinner parties – none of which we'd been invited to. Then, right by the lobby, Dad suddenly spotted Reese and her new husband, Jim Toth.

(Ugh! I knew it. She'd found someone new.)

Omar rushed over to say hello, and Reese was as sweet as could be. 'Where's Uggie?' she asked.

'He's in his room. I'll go get him!' Omar told her, but she and her husband were heading for a limo to take them to the *Vanity Fair*/Bloomberg after-party. By the time he'd hurried back down in the elevator with me in his arms, they'd gone.

I could hardly believe it. I could pick up the scent of her peachy skin, but she was nowhere to be seen.

'Don't worry, buddy,' Dad told me, sensing my distress. 'We'll find her.'

Heartsick with longing, I wandered outside with him so I could stand where Reese had recently stood and take a moment. Then Dad got talking to a couple of men who were huge fans of mine.

'You want to go to the *Vanity Fair* party?' one asked, stroking me under my chin. 'Come with us, and we'll try to get you in!'

It was raining, and we didn't have a limo, so we walked the four blocks to the party. Wide-eyed and straining forward, I zigzagged after Reese's scent as we followed the two burly humans. They led us to the entrance of the grandest house I had ever seen.

'What is this place?' Mercy asked breathlessly.

'The French Ambassador's residence,' came the reply.

*Ce n'est pas possible!* What was it with me and the French? They seemed to bring me only good luck. I held out a small vestige of hope.

When we got in line to go in, we could see security guards at the door asking for tickets. We were very much *sans* tickets, and our companions began to fear that we wouldn't be allowed in.

'Tickets?' the guard asked Omar, when we got to the front of the line.

'This is Uggie from *The Artist*,' he said, holding me up like an Oscar statuette.

There was a slight pause and then the guard said, 'Okay, go!' and waved us in.

Yes!

My ears were up, and all my senses were tuned to Reese, but there was no time to look for her. I was immediately swamped with people wanting to meet me. I performed a few stunts for my adoring fans, and everyone crowded around.

'Uggie's the biggest star here,' people told Dad time and again. *Vanity Fair* declared me its favourite guest. Colin Powell, the former US Secretary of State, hurried over and asked Omar to take a photograph of him with me, for his granddaughters. 'We're all huge fans!' he said.

Posing with the Colombian long-coat
Sofia Vergara at the *Vanity Fair* party.

Goldie Hawn came up to smother me in kisses. She smelled delicious and was as light and lovely as she appeared on TV. I could have licked her face all night. If I'd only met her before Reese, who knows what could have happened?

George Clooney was there, of course, handsome as ever. He flashed me that dazzling smile of his that made me want to go back to my canine dentist for more treatment.

A senior representative of the French Embassy had his photograph taken with me and said it was 'the greatest honour' to have me as their guest.

*Incroyable!*

I was lapping up all the attention when my little wet nose began to twitch and the hairs on the back of my neck suddenly stood on end. Pausing with one paw in the air, I caught a memory on the wind.

Sure enough, walking towards me with a 1,000-megawatt smile on her face was Ms Witherspoon, in an elegant black gown and turquoise earrings. As always, she carried her beauty with such grace.

'Hello Uggie!' she cried, and then she kissed me.

It was a heart-stopping moment. If Dad hadn't been holding me tight at that point, I think I might have passed out from sheer bliss.

She and her new mate (grrr!) chatted with Mom and Dad for quite a while. I heard Reese say how 'amazing' I was in *The Artist*, as I sighed happily. Dad asked after Hank and Nashville (her lucky hounds), and Mom spoke to her about the baby Reese was expecting in a few months' time.

All I could do was stare at her giddily, and with envy in my heart. My very own screen goddess looked radiant, with her skin as creamy as a magnolia. I could only be happy for her. Giving her husband a perfunctory lick, I decided not to hold a grudge against the human who was obviously taking such good care of her.

Dad took loads of photos, and when she was smiling at the camera, I managed to snuggle right next to her face and lick her more than I could ever have hoped for.

Reese loved me!

Showing Reese Witherspoon the
meaning of French kissing after the
White House Correspondents Dinner.

She hadn't forgotten me!
I would always have a place in her heart.
As she would in mine.

**40**

IN THE END, IT'S NOT GOING TO
MATTER HOW MANY BREATHS YOU TOOK
BUT HOW MANY MOMENTS TOOK
YOUR BREATH AWAY.
*Shing Xiong*

**M**y glittering night in Washington DC, was one of the greatest of my life. It surpassed skateboarding, water-skiing, Binge-Gate, and even my experiences on the set of my two favourite movies.

Maybe it was because I was so much older and wiser and finally starting to appreciate the important things in life, such as love and friendship. As I began to snore gently on my luxurious hotel bed that night, I had never felt more contented.

I could tell that Mom and Dad had enjoyed our visit to the capital as much as I had. It was an event they would undoubtedly talk about for the rest of their lives. I was so glad they had shared the experience with me, and I was never more grateful for Omar's presence at my side. He'd been my shadow and my friend throughout my breakneck romp through life, and whenever I saw his eyes glisten with pride, I knew that I'd done right by him, too.

The animal-loving kid from Colombia, who'd laid on his belly on the roof of his childhood home, dreaming of going to America one day, had ended up going places with me that he could never have imagined in a million years.

He'd lived through a hurricane and a recession; he'd found true love with Mercy and become a father to precious Terry. Throughout everything he had faced, he'd remained steadfastly loyal to his animals and devoted to me, from the day I burst naughtily into his world.

From our earliest days on the Santa Monica streets working for a few crumpled dollars, and through endless hours of one-to-one coaching, we'd supported each other through good times and bad. After our humble beginnings in commercials and a few low-budget movies, we'd faced rejection after rejection before the planets realigned.

We two didn't know it then, but our coming together had forged us a star-studded destiny that would lead us to pad along some of the most famous red carpets in the world. We'd been given a unique opportunity to play our part in a movie that brought such joy to the world and gave me fame beyond the realms of fantasy.

That funny little foreign picture had then gone on to win all those awards and become one of the classic movies of all time. Thanks to its incredible success, we'd been able to promote the invaluable work of coaches such as Omar and the dedication of animal actors, such as myself. We'd travelled the globe together and been hugged and kissed by the greats of our time.

Taking a well-earned rest in my
so-called 'retirement'.

Omar had changed my life, and now I had changed his, too. He had done a fantastic job of keeping me humble along the way. Even when I was told I was to be given one of the highest honours Hollywood could give an actor – the chance to be the first dog to cast my pawprints in concrete outside Grauman's Chinese Theatre – Omar never let me forget that I was anything other than a family pet. The day my prints were immortalised (25 June) was declared 'Uggie Day' by the city fathers, but I was just an ordinary member of Omar's pack (which continued to expand with the arrival of Puff, a sweet but over-possessive Pomeranian).

My collars and awards were put away in a cupboard, and my gift baskets were shared with the rest of the guys at home. Omar encouraged me in my charity work and spent time with me at pet shows, hospices, children's hospitals, and homes for the elderly, where people often said that meeting me was a dream come true.

'Uggie's such a joy! He spreads love and happiness wherever he goes,' one young woman in a wheelchair told him, as she cuddled me at one of the many events we attended. For her great insight into what was surely my true purpose in life, I licked her face sincerely.

'You always light up a room, buddy!' Omar would tell me, his eyes shining.

Omar and Mercy had nursed me through my surgery and charted the gradual progression of my neurological condition. He'd paid for every possible kind of treatment for me and had become my fiercest protector and most faithful companion. My rest periods had become sacrosanct, and I even had personal protection whenever I needed it.

Mostly, Dad had taught me how deeply humans love. He had somehow filled my little doggy heart with such feelings for him and the rest of my family, that they often overwhelmed my canine sensibilities.

Whenever my hour as a player on the stage runs out (and I hope for many more happy dog years by Omar's side), I know that his love for me will enable him to make that bravest of decisions. He and he alone will declare, 'Okay, Uggie. That's a wrap!' and let me have that long, last nap.

Only then will I skateboard up that great red carpet in the sky. I like to think that Extreme Pete and Andy will be up there and game for a little light squirrel chasing. Maybe Gizmo will regard me with amused indifference, and without unsheathing his claws.

I hardly dare hope that the likes of Rin Tin Tin or Moose might be waiting to say hello, and – who knows? – maybe acknowledge my contribution to the canine canon with a sniff of my celebrity butt.

I have no regrets.

My only hope is that long after my paws no longer tread this earth, I will still be remembered as a little artist, with a big heart.

# ACKNOWLEDGEMENTS

I wouldn't be where I am today if it weren't for my business partner and acting coach Omar von Muller, an extraordinary human and the best buddy a dog could hope for. His diligence, professionalism, and patience paved the way for me to do some of my finest work. I dedicate my many awards to him.

His mate Mercy and their pup – my 'sister' Terry – were also loving and loyal companions. I appreciated every cuddle, bath, and slice of pizza. They helped keep me grounded amidst all the Hollywood hype and reminded me that, in the words of Brad Pitt, fame can be a bitch.

My biographer Wendy Holden exhibited many admirable canine qualities (especially dogged persistence). I am grateful to her for putting my thoughts and memories into human language and forgive her for favouring spaniels. Alan Nevins proved to be a Rottweiler of an agent, as well as a fine judge of character in his choice of terriers as housemates.

Having sniffed out a perfect pack of publishers, I was delighted by their Labrador loyalty to this memoir, especially Carole Tonkinson and Victoria McGeown at HarperCollins in the UK, Jennifer Bergstrom and Jeremie Ruby-Strauss at Gallery in the US, and Laurent Laffont and team at Editions Jean-Claude Lattès in France.

I was fortunate enough to work with some great actors, as well as many good humans, and one of those was the inimitable

Jean Dujardin, who proved to be the finest fellow thespian on *The Artist* and a true exponent of *joie de vivre*. I applaud him for doing so well in his quest to learn American dog.

Michel Hazanavicius deserves my thanks for writing such a great piece of theatre and one that gave me a chance to showcase my array of acting talents. Throughout filming, Monsieur H. was open to all my artistic suggestions and was unusually biddable for a director.

I'd especially like to thank all those agencies who signed me and gave me the opportunity to hone my craft. They included Jungle Exotics, Gentle Jungle, and Hollywood Animals. Sarah Clifford from Animal Savvy (who not only recommended me for *The Artist* but also helped me through some of its most challenging scenes) deserves a special mention, as does Toby Rose, founder of the Palm Dog Awards in Cannes. Oh, and I need to bark a special and most grateful hello to Rupert Thorpe, Hollywood photographer to the stars.

I was also grateful to the Movieline website for its 'Consider Uggie' campaign, and to the thousands of fans who followed me on my various social networking sites. Thanks, too, to Dog News Daily for my Golden Collar Award, and to the American Humane Association for my Pawscar. Those accolades meant more to me than I could say.

I am, of course, indebted to the talented cast, crew, wranglers, make-up artists, and caterers on *The Artist*, as well as to the Weinstein Company for the sausages.

I lick each of your faces, truly.

# PICTURE CREDITS